Quarterly Essay

CONTENTS

Quarterly Essay is published four times a year by Black Inc.

ISBN 1 86395 1474

Subscriptions (4 issues): $46.95 a year within Australia incl. GST (Institutional subs. $52.95). Outside Australia $74.95. Payment may be made by Mastercard, Visa or Bankcard, or by cheque made out to Schwartz Publishing. Payment includes postage and handling.

Subscribe online at **www.blackincbooks.com** or fill out and post the subscription form on the last page of this essay.

Correspondence and subscriptions should be addressed to the Editor at:
Black Inc.
Level 5, 289 Flinders Lane
Melbourne VIC 3000 Australia
Phone: 61 3 9654 2000
Fax: 61 3 9654 2290
Email: quarterlyessay@blackincbooks.com
http://www.blackincbooks.com

Editor: Peter Craven
Management: Silvia Kwon
Assistant Editor: Chris Feik
Production Coordinator: Sophy Williams
Publicity: Meredith Kelly
Design: Guy Mirabella
Printer: McPherson's Printing Group
Author photograph: Jennifer Herold
Front cover image: AAP Image/ Laura Friezer

Quarterly Essay aims to present significant contributions to political, intellectual and cultural debate. It is a magazine in extended pamphlet form and by publishing in each issue a single writer at a length of at least 20,000 words we hope to mediate between the limitations of the newspaper column, where there is the danger that evidence and argument can be swallowed up by the form, and the kind of full-length study of a subject where the only readership is a necessarily specialised one. *Quarterly Essay* aims for the attention of the committed general reader. Although it is a periodical which wants subscribers, each number of the journal is the length of a short book because we want our writers to have the opportunity to speak to the broadest possible audience without condescension or populist short-cuts. *Quarterly Essay* wants to get away from the tyranny that space limits impose in contemporary journalism and we give our essayists the space to express the evidence for their views and those who disagree with them the chance to reply at whatever length is necessary. *Quarterly Essay* will not be confined to politics but is centrally concerned with it. We are not interested in occupying any particular point on the political map and we hope to bring our readership the widest range of political and cultural opinion which is compatible with truth-telling, style and command of the essay form.

INTRODUCTION

During the lead-up to the last election when Kim Beazley gave his backing to John Howard's *Border Protection Act* (blocking the asylum seekers) the story went round that John Button was unhappy with the Labor Party he had served for many years. It was a moment when Labor True Believers of all descriptions were going through the dark night of the soul from which they still have not recovered: they went on to vote Green or informal or to cast their vote for a party in which they had ceased to believe.

That was just what you would expect from the "chats", whether they were enlightened captains of industry or students, because the broad coalition of liberal-minded intelligentsia who had always believed that the gap between Labor and the conservatives, whether great or small, was the gap in which we lived, had just seen that myth exploded as Beazley took his saunter towards the moral dustbin of Labor history. But for John Button to be outraged meant that some kind of writing was on the wall.

John Button has always been one of the great agnostic stalwarts of the Labor Party, a man who has kept his faith in the continuities between the Labor parties of Curtin and Chifley and Whitlam and Hawke but who was sceptical of the orthodoxies that often seemed to trail along with them.

John Button helped Gough Whitlam purge the Left in Victoria in the 1960s and he managed a distinguished political career that culminated with the Labor leadership in the Senate without being beholden to the factions of the party. But, at the same time, Button was never quite one of the new-style radical conservative Labor technocrats. As Minister for Industry in the Hawke/Keating years, he was the man at the coalface when the Australian economy was modernised and deregulated (he saw the factories close and the jobs go) but he was never a doctrinal marketeer.

All of which feeds into *Beyond Belief: What Future for Labor?*, which represents one of the coolest and most disheartening accounts of a great political party this country has seen. This is the Australian Labor Party seen from the perspective of an elder statesman who has an absolute belief (however tacitly stated) in the moral superiority of the Labor cause but who wonders whether the ALP will ever achieve government again and who distinctly implies that in its present state it is not fit for it.

Beyond Belief is a portrait of a moribund political party that has been in serious need of structural reform for at least a generation, which has lost any sense of its function as a progressive socially democratic party of at least the nominal Left, but which has always been the party that implements change in Australia.

Not that Button has any time for the Coalition now in government. He sees it – right down to what might be construed as John Howard's achievements – as essentially reactive rather than initiating. And what the Liberal Party has been reacting against in the last century or so of its existence has been the impulse towards reform in the Labor Party.

Part of Button's quite dire critique of Labor's strategy in the period when it thought it might amble into office was that it developed an invisible attitude to policy initiatives, almost as if it could gain government by the essentially conservative tactic of not distinguishing itself from a conservative government.

In Button's view this left Beazley's Labor Party threadbare when it was suddenly faced with a moral or political crisis, as Howard went smiling into the election on a wave of patriotic alarmism.

Beyond Belief is not a mere post-mortem on Beazley's advisers or his ill-advised campaign. Button is just as interested in taking him to task for his lack of pugnacity in reforming the party and ensuring that the best candidates went before the electorate.

But this is not a *Quarterly Essay* that's interested in pointing the finger at individuals. It cannot be because John Button's indictment is too structural and too thoroughgoing. It is a portrait of a party that has lost any ability to muster grassroots support, which is characterised by factions that stand for nothing but the perpetuation of their own power (mere operational warlords effecting strategy in an ideological void) and unions that debilitate the Labor Party while gaining nothing for themselves or their constituencies.

It's a portrait of a political party that has narrowed its own social basis and in the process lost sight of Chifley's still valid ideal of the light on the hill. In his quiet way Button is nowhere more devastating than in his account of how the Labor Party has professionalised itself to such an extent that it can actually look like a nepotised clerisy or at least a set of family concerns.

John Button is at one level nostalgic for a more red-blooded Labor Party where an ex-shearer like Mick Young could mix with intellectuals and lawyers and still keep the common touch so essential to political communication, and he is very shrewd in pointing out that the innovations in Labor government, whether of the reformist Whitlam variety or of the professional and managerial Hawke/Keating variety, did not come from politicians who went through nothing but the strait gait of Labor careerism.

There are moments throughout *Beyond Belief* when the reader – and perhaps all the more so if she is a True Believer – will want to exclaim, "What do they know of Labor who only Labor know?"

John Button knows a lot of other things – which is one reason why he can speak appreciatively of Menzies and even of Howard – and it is his breadth of knowledge that makes him fearful of a parliamentary party made up of hereditary heirs and tyros of the factions and people who stand for the perpetuation of power rather than its proper use.

He is not, of course, a simplistic True Believer, however much he cleaves to the "truth" of that Labor light. John Button is impatient of anyone who wants to dispute the sane tough-minded side of economic rationalism even though he has no faith in the dogma of the myopic econocrat adherents.

This is a *Quarterly Essay* by a man who has spent a lifetime in politics and who commands the respect of both sides of it. It is an essay by someone who refuses, on principle, to believe in the heart-warming sentimentalities of political mythology but who nonetheless believes that the Labor Party should turn itself into something worth believing in because faith of a rational kind has to be part of the political equation and New Believers are the key to any future worth having.

One of the ironies of this wise, sceptical essay by one of the great realists of Australian politics is that it takes a figure like John Button to remind the ALP that it is, at the end of the day, a party with a commitment to progressive reform which takes its raison d'être from that fact. He makes it quite clear that he believes the Labor Party has imperilled itself by ignoring just that mandate.

Along the way John Button has penetrating things to say about Tony Blair and Third Wayism, about the Greens and the Democrats and about such thinkers in the Labor Party as Mark Latham and Lindsay Tanner.

This is an urgent essay, written at the very time that Bob Hawke and Neville Wran, those old-timers, are preparing their report about how the Labor Party can rejuvenate itself. John Button is himself an old-timer but he has an impassioned sense of how the party that he pledged his faith to when he was young has been allowed to rot and maybe even perish.

The fact that John Button can raise the spectre of that possibility – one which would bewilder minds on all sides of Australian politics – is a testament to his tough-mindedness and courage.

This is a brave essay, full of devastating implication, by the insider who has written the most vivid eyewitness accounts we have of Australian politics. It is the cold-eyed testament of a born politician who is also one of nature's writers and one of the things it testifies to – in the face of what may be a wave that will hurl the Labor Party into the oblivion of history

– is that the Labor Party does represent a light that has always shone in the face of every skullduggery and self-serving opportunism, including its own.

Peter Craven

FOREWORD

This essay is about the political culture and organisation of the Australian Labor Party in 2002. The culture is inward-looking and incestuous, the organisation is old and sclerotic. They work hand in glove: the hand of the political culture is comfortable in the old glove of the organisation. Imagining significant change is disconcerting, yet change has to come, and most ALP members know it.

The essay is not about personalities. Most people will do their best in the environment in which they find themselves. But sometimes, with the best will in the world, the imagination is constrained by illusory ambitions and an innate fear of rocking the boat.

As a member of the ALP for nearly fifty years, I have experienced most of the party's lows and highs during that time. My sense is that the party is at an all-time low in its morale, ideas and democratic participation. Creativity in Australian politics requires a mixture of healthy scepticism and guarded hope. The ALP, if it is to reach highs in the future, has to embark on an exercise requiring imagination, courage and goodwill. It has to reform itself.

For eighteen years in my Canberra office I kept a quotation from the American commentator C. Hartley Grattan on the wall behind my desk:

> It has struggled with every handicap to which political parties are heir. It has been burdened with careerists, turncoats, hypocrites, outright scoundrels, stuffy functionaries devoid of sense and imagination, bellowing enemies of critical intelligence, irritatingly self-righteous clowns bent on enforcing suburban points of view, pussy-footers, demagogues, stooges for hostile outside groups and interests, aged and decaying hacks and ordinary blatherskites. Every political party falls heir to these. But it has outlived them all and still stands for something: it stands for a social democratic Australia.

This was written in 1942. It contains both scepticism and guarded hope. It's hard to see that Australian politics has changed a lot since then. The ALP has outlived another sixty years or so of handicaps and electoral reverses. Whether it can go on doing so is a matter of conjecture. What it has to be sure about is what it stands for as Australia enters another century.

Four and a quarter million Australians voted for the Labor Party in the election of November 2001. They were betting on a hope rather than a certainty. As the only party capable of making real social change, of making the country a better one for all its citizens, the ALP is too important to languish in the past and fall victim to a narrow political culture. If the hopes of its supporters are to be realised, it has to be outward looking, guided by the idea of a social democratic Australia.

It is to point out what might be possible, as distinct from immediately achievable, that this essay has been written.

John Button

BEYOND BELIEF

What Future for Labor?

John Button

One night in April 2002 I attended a local ALP branch meeting. I don't attend regularly any more. Branch meetings remind me of the weary remark of Prime Minister John Curtin: "I am a veteran of 10,000 conferences."

Eight people attended the meeting. Two of them were members of parliament, one federal and one state. Because there was no quorum it was decided not to adopt the minutes of the previous meeting. This was a proper decision, strictly in accordance with the rules. Local branches always obey the procedural rules.

The meeting was held in the grey besser-brick office of the state member of parliament. Inside it is well arranged; neat and functional. Filing cabinets line one side of the main room. There's a rack full of brochures, a copy machine in one corner. Like most offices, the atmosphere is cold rather than cool.

Posters and electoral maps on the walls hint at the condition of the body politic, like charts and illustrations in the waiting room of a medical clinic explaining the onset of arthritis or osteoporosis. Eight small tables with steel legs and laminex tops are arranged side by side to make one big table large enough for a family of eight.

We sat, face to face, across the table. Lindsay Tanner, the federal member, spoke about the last election and then about the problems besetting the ALP. He said the political "trendlines" were bad. The party had a very low membership in outer suburbia: members felt ignored and couldn't see the value of membership. "We have", he said, "a good brand name but a bad product." He sounded like a visiting clinician describing the effects of chronic fatigue syndrome. There were, he warned, no quick fixes, no wonder drugs. It was an honest analysis but depressing.

When the parliamentarians left, a discussion took place among those who remained. An Englishwoman told us about the euphoria in the British Labour Party when the Blair government was elected. People nodded, trying to imagine what it was like. I think she was trying to cheer us up. Another woman said she'd felt depressed before the meeting but now she felt worse. She explained how difficult it was trying to interest her neighbours and work colleagues in supporting the ALP. Two longstanding members said this was probably the last year in which they'd take out a membership ticket. They'd had enough of feeling "irrelevant". One woman, who'd transferred from Tasmania, said she'd stay on and I believed her.

The meeting took about an hour and a half. We shuffled out onto the footpath like people who'd been to a doctor and received bad news. We'd seen the X-rays. I walked home along streets laid out in the first half of the nineteenth century, past gentrified working-men's cottages with BMWs parked outside them and past houses where Labor families still live, families who don't come to meetings any more. I walked on pavements trodden by a Labor prime minister, Jimmy Scullin, and by other Labor MPs whose names are part of the history of the party. I paused on a street corner where in the winter of 1955 people clustered in the cold and listened to a young and idealistic Jim Cairns talk about political ideas and social values.

The branch whose meeting I'd attended has a long history. It used to meet in the town hall and if there weren't forty or fifty people present it was a bad night. I went to the meeting because the branch president sent an email around reminding members of his football team's challenge to its supporters: "If you don't come, why should we?"

Was all that past effort worthwhile? Of course it was. But at the start of the twenty-first century, the ALP enjoys a history of which it is proud but which has limited relevance to the future. There is a legacy of some good governments and some not so good, a rich folklore and some extraordinary achievements. Perhaps the ALP's greatest past success has been in broadening the agenda of Australian political life, its ability throughout most of its history to push the Conservatives into the role of the parties who resist change.

Australia's parliamentary system has survived for one century and may, or may not, survive the next in its present form. For a hundred years it has depended on two major parties, Conservative and Labor, in turn providing government and opposition. Sometimes the two-party system seems tired and incestuous, and its achievements are not widely acknowledged. Political stability is one of them. The alternative is a multi-party system, that well-known recipe for instability.

In recent years a growing number of voters have turned to other political parties: One Nation (for the disaffected), the Democrats (advocating "change politics", something better than the present) and the Greens (who describe themselves as the party of "thinking" voters). Two of these parties are on the progressive side of politics. None of them is capable of forming a government, now or in any foreseeable future. None of them has to decide what, as a government, it would really do.

Voters can sense the fatigue of the two-party system. They yearn for new ideas, fresh visions of what Australia might be. Ultimately they have little choice and they return the party that they believe best represents their interests. That's why the Coalition is in government in 2002. With its history of being the major party of social change, the ALP can call on strong residual community sentiment. That's why it gets such a relatively large vote. But sentiment is not going to sustain it: voters want a real choice and Labor no longer offers them one. The ALP is seen as a pale alternative to the Coalition. It is incapable of embracing and speaking for the divergent progressive groups in the community. It has been unable to respond effectively to new aspirations. It no longer represents contemporary Australia. It may not even represent its members any more: its national body has become an offshore island adrift from the rest of the party, inaccessible to its rank and file, a barren and rocky outcrop untouched by new ideas.

When the Labor government of Paul Keating was returned to office in 1993, Keating described the result as a victory for the "True Believers". What did he mean by that? He meant "the people who in difficult times had kept the faith", those who always voted Labor, who believed that a Labor government was always better than a Conservative one.

True Believers talk of the wartime governments of John Curtin and the post-war government of Ben Chifley as the high-water mark of Labor's twentieth century. Both Curtin and Chifley had exceptional ability; both had their roots in the traditional working class and had come to politics through the trade union movement. Both presided over competent governments, although Chifley's prime ministership ended in 1949 as a result of political misjudgements. The careers of both men were characterised by integrity and humility. Their lives and their examples have nourished the soul of the ALP ever since. Like the ghost of Hamlet's father, Chifley's gruff voice incants to the True Believers, "Remember me."

Insofar as there is discussion of ideas and beliefs in the ALP, it has always turned on the issue of the values of socialism or social democracy and how those values are best implemented in a changing world. These are complex issues that can be made highly technical by dedicated bores, which is why so many Labor people admire Chifley's simply stated vision, uncluttered by political jargon, of the light on the hill:

> I try to think of the labour movement, not as putting an extra sixpence into somebody's pocket, or making somebody Prime Minister or Premier, but as a movement bringing something better to the people, better standards of living, greater happiness to the mass of the people. We have a great objective – the light on the hill – which we aim to reach by working for the betterment of mankind not only here but anywhere we may give a helping hand.

There is no reason why these words cannot continue to express the heart and soul of the ALP. But they must do so in a way that is contemporary and relevant, not lost in the mists of Labor retrospect. Perhaps the fundamental question is this: can a political party organised for the early twentieth century, that has grown content with recycled ideas, compete for influence and power in the twenty-first century?

In a party dedicated to change, change from within is sometimes the hardest thing to achieve. But if it is to regain government with a meaningful reform agenda, Labor has no choice. There is understandably much sentiment about "True Believers". They're the link with history. But new believers are the key to the future.

On the morning of Sunday 11 November last year, I walked down to the corner store to buy the newspapers. A man stopped me in the street for a chat. "I thought your mate did well last night," he said. "Made a dignified speech." I nodded. "That's something coming from me," he added. "I'm an extreme right-winger." At certain times even extreme right-wingers can be magnanimous. This bloke, along with many Australians, liked Kim Beazley. Now that Beazley had been beaten, he liked him even more.

Beazley had conceded the federal election to the Coalition at about ten o'clock the night before. It was indeed a dignified speech, and a difficult one to make for a man who was for some time justifiably encouraged to believe that he would become prime minister. He congratulated John Howard and hoped for better things to come. "Bleak Angels" and "Good Angels" contended in the country's nature. Problem issues such as health care and education would not go away. He thanked his supporters, the candidates and his family. Then he thanked his advisers. This was generous. He had nothing in particular to thank them for.

The newspapers added little to the television and radio commentaries of the night before. Just the cold reality of print. Hard copy. On the surface it was a "no change" election, but only on the surface.

The final result showed a 2.26 per cent swing in primary votes against the ALP. This doesn't sound much, but the two-party preferred vote (the primary vote plus the second preferences of minor parties) was the biggest swing to a government since 1966. Labor gained just one seat – in Ballarat, Victoria – and lost two in New South Wales, one in Queensland and one in Western Australia. Its primary vote exceeded the Coalition's in only two of the six states (Victoria and Tasmania) and in the Northern Territory. In Queensland Labor retained 7 seats out of a total of 27, in Western Australia 7 out of 15 and in South Australia 3 out of 12. In New South Wales, once regarded as a stronghold, the ALP was left with 20 seats out of 50. Most devastating of all, the ALP recorded its lowest national primary vote since 1931. These were some of the key figures for Labor hidden in the so-called "no change" election.

On the night of 10 November, when the result became clear, Peter Costello observed that there would be "a lot of soul searching in the ALP". Nobody in the ALP remarked that there were grounds for soul searching in the Liberal Party, even though defeated One Nation leader Pauline Hanson said in her own breathtakingly understated epitaph, "I'm pleased with what I have achieved. I've seen the Liberal Party pick up a lot of the policies and issues that I have spoken about over the last few years."

Labor's soul searching is destined to take time. One former federal minister, Duncan Kerr, said the party had lost its soul altogether. In the weeks after the election a rush of remedies was proposed. Three front-benchers called for an end to "the 60–40 rule", which enshrines union majorities of 60 per cent at party conferences. Others drew attention to the lack of internal democracy in the party, decay within the grassroots organization, and the need for a more open and inclusive party. The New South Wales Premier, Bob Carr, called for a purge of dead wood from the ranks of federal parliamentarians in New South Wales, the need for "deft retirements and new talent". As a prudent premier he confined his remarks to his own state. He might have gone further.

Media commentators and political analysts conducted their own post-mortems. Within a few days the key Labor strategists and some commentators had decided that the ALP's demise resulted from the dreaded plague *Tampa* released by the wicked apothecary John Howard and his scheming assistants. Others were less certain. Later, other forensic experts gave more considered opinions. Some of them said, "The ALP is not dead. It is in a deep coma and has been for some time. Perhaps it can be woken up." The veteran electoral analyst Professor Mackerras arrived with his pendulum which, of course, swings both ways. This was comforting because it can always swing back.

The November election was merely the lowest point of a year that in retrospect will be seen as an *annus horribilis*, not this time for the Queen but for the membership of the ALP. It was not so much that the election was lost and hopes dashed. These things happen; incumbents have an advantage, in this election cleverly exploited. The ALP has lost federal elections before, and more particularly failed to win them. No, it was what happened, or failed to happen, in the year before the election that sapped the morale of party members.

If November was Labor's lowest point in 2001, the highest point was probably May. Then the opinion polls were running strongly in Labor's favour and there was a lot of talk about the "unlosable election". Labor had won two state elections that year and a by-election in the federal Queensland seat of Ryan; it now held power in every state except South Australia. On 3 May newspapers reported the leaking of a memo from Shane Stone, then federal president of the Liberal Party, who complained to Prime Minister John Howard that the public saw the government as "mean, tricky and out of touch".

On 8 May a book, *True Believers*, celebrating the centenary of the Parliamentary Labor Party, was launched at Parliament House, Melbourne. It is a comprehensive account of Labor's triumphs and failings during the hundred years since the party's first federal parliamentary meeting in Melbourne.

The celebrations continued that night with a gala dinner at the Melbourne Park Function Centre. It was a night on which, as Tony Walker wrote in the *Financial Review*, "Labor and its foot soldiers are starting to behave as if Ben Chifley's Light Upon the Hill is within their reach." Nearly everyone who should have been there was there, including three former prime ministers – Whitlam, Hawke and Keating – former leader Bill Hayden, five Labor premiers and a happy crowd of past and present members of parliament. The 1600 guests dined on chicken artichoke and bell pepper salad dressed with Ligurian olive oil and McLaren Vale olives, a choice of King Dory with roma tomato and *parmentier* potato or herb crusted sirloin with sweet potato medallions and grain mustard jus, and lime meringue pie splashed with raspberry and chocolate sauce.

The wine flowed freely.

Between courses the guests were treated to two very professional video presentations of Labor's colourful history in the first and second halves of the twentieth century, and speeches from the three former prime ministers and Kim Beazley. The speeches were brief and well crafted. Gough Whitlam, ageing but unbowed, indulged the audience with some vintage Whitlam wit and erudition. "Men and women of Australia," he began, evoking the euphoria of his election campaign opening in 1972. He reminded his audience that in the late 1960s he'd had to grapple with a culture of opposition-mindedness in the Victorian ALP, repeating the now famous phrase, "only the impotent are pure." Paul Keating, too, was witty but also thoughtful. He described the founding fathers of Australian federation as lawyers and businessmen, "mostly old forelock tuggers", who had given Australia a British century. Would we have in the twenty-first century an Australian century or an American century? "The Conservatives, you can bet on this, will forelock tug their way to Washington, and our future as an independent country, as a republic in Asia, in our neighbourhood, will be lost."

Bob Hawke, the closest to Beazley and widely regarded as his mentor, gave a different kind of speech. He referred to the ALP's "seeming paradox – the simultaneous commitment to constancy and change" and illustrated it by examples from "the vivid tapestry" of Labor's past. Much of his speech was devoted to saying what a Beazley government would do. Some of the audience were relieved to hear it. People kept glancing at Beazley, whose face was fixed in a cautious smile. One sensed that Hawke's acute political instincts had told him that if the forthcoming election was to be won the ALP needed a higher public profile, an articulation of a different and bolder vision. If this was a signal, it didn't seem to work.

Kim Beazley spoke last. It was a good political speech and it focused on the theme of the evening's celebrations, Labour's proud traditions. He invoked the spirit of Ben Chifley. He criticised the Howard government. He was cautious about policies. He warned against arrogance, refraining from observing that he was surrounded by it in Canberra. The speeches were received with rapturous applause. Across the table from me, Keating seemed lost in thought. While Hawke spoke, he scribbled notes for his speech on a piece of paper. The wine was passed around, memories and regrets exchanged. It was a happy family gathering. True Believers love their history. And for one night, they loved each other.

As the lime meringue pies were polished off, queues of people clamouring for autographs on their copy of *True Believers* formed at the tables of the former leaders. Slowly and reluctantly the crowd dispersed into a balmy Melbourne night. The Labor Party seemed to have recaptured its spirit. Power was again within its grasp. And so the cruise ship sailed towards the iceberg.

With their celebration, the ALP had stolen the centenary show. John Howard resents Labor's iconographic history and on this occasion he was annoyed enough to comment. Beazley was opportunistic in identifying himself with the Chifley tradition, Howard said: "I didn't agree with much of what Ben Chifley stood for, but at least Ben Chifley stood for something."

Did this dark remark resonate with Labor's rank and file? Throughout 2001 ALP members constantly wondered what a Labor government would do to address particular issues of public concern. Apart from generalised waffle about commitment to education and health and rolling back the GST, there were no satisfactory answers from the parliamentary leadership to any of the questions, big or small. The rank and file were hardly in a position to trumpet the advantages of a Labor government. The only honest answer they could give to the undecided or curious voter was "wait and see."

Labor had decided to steal the small target strategy from Howard's 1996 campaign. It's the Christopher Robin posture – get into bed and curl up small and nobody knows you're there at all. It sits naturally with a party of reaction but uncomfortably with a party of progressive reform. Focus groups conducted in twenty-eight marginal electorates had confirmed the government's unpopularity, but focus groups are about following, not leadership. At best they "provide the intelligence required to fool the people at least some of the time". In this case they fooled the ALP's strategists.

Nonetheless, in spite of the headlines and euphoria, doubts lingered about Labor's small target strategy. In the Shadow Cabinet four and sometimes five shadow ministers voiced these doubts, but this remained a well-kept secret.

If any ALP policy received a high public profile it was the rollback of the GST, a policy for which the government could claim some sort of mandate from the 1998 election. Over the next few months, senior opposition figures hammered the GST, calling it the source of Australia's economic woes. The GST was certainly unpopular, and it had been introduced sloppily by the government; yet, in News Polls taken between January 2000 and September 2001, five polls out of six showed the Coalition comfortably heading Labor as the best party to handle taxation. If the polls were right, then tax, even the GST, was not well chosen as a battleground.

"Rollback" was a pathetic policy from the beginning. Apart from giving the impression that the Opposition was intent on fighting the elections of 1993 and 1998 rather than the one at hand, it also sought the best of both worlds – capitalising on the unpopularity of the GST while doing little about it except for making a feeble and vague commitment. It was rightly seen as cynical and hypocritical. A progressive political party should roll forward, not back, was the observation I made to Simon Crean at the Grand Final Breakfast in September 2000.

The policy detracted from the ALP's ability to put more money into health and education and so distinguish its priorities from those of the government. And in mid-year Howard had a bit of rollback himself, softening the hardline image with a series of handouts to the potentially disaffected. By the time the details of Labor's rollback were announced it had all the impact of a discreetly smothered burp.

In the months leading up to the election the ALP had little to say about unemployment or the quality of jobs. No mention was made of growing income inequality; GST rollback was the "centrepiece". "Knowledge Nation", a vision for a better educated society – which properly refined and packaged in terms of its significance might have been a centrepiece – was announced and then backed away from, largely because of its easily mocked spaghetti and meatballs diagram. This was all small target stuff, which made it difficult to explain what the Opposition believed. And by mid-year it was hard to detect much enthusiasm for what people imagined Labor's policies to be, certainly not the sort of enthusiasm engendered by Whitlam in 1972 or Hawke in 1983.

In August I wrote to a senior shadow minister:

> I'm afraid that among the opinion-forming, educated ("chattering") class there is little enthusiasm for the Labor Party. This lot is to be found in universities, sections of the public service and more enlightened industrialists. They don't like Howard and are not attracted by us. Whether this is considered relevant by party "strategists" or not I don't know. All I do know is that this section of the electorate was there for Gough, Hawke to some extent and Keating, but it is not there now. I tend to attribute this not so much to the unhappy Kimbo as to poor nurturing, perhaps laziness, by some of your shadow ministerial colleagues. I don't expect any comment on this but offer this opinion for what it is worth.

Discretion and solidarity are important weapons in the armoury of a shadow minister. I was grateful for a polite but non-committal letter of acknowledgement.

In the upshot the media concluded that there was little difference between the policies of the major parties on the issues of education, health, defence, aged care and the environment. So did the voters.

After the election debacle some people in the party blamed the *Tampa* and September 11. But the simple fact is that the ALP had not built an adequate policy profile or built up sufficient enthusiasm and respect for its style of politics. Without these, it had no hope of differentiating its position on refugees and asylum seekers from the government's when this became the key issue of the election. Wayne Swan, widely regarded as a key Labor strategist, put it this way:

> I want to be clear that without *Tampa* and September 11, I believe Labor would have prevailed in a hard-fought campaign. But we must also acknowledge that before *Tampa* and September 11 there was a loss of impetus in our drive towards victory. Our private polling in April showed us ahead, but too much of the swing was being driven by preferences from minor party voters, rather than a groundswell of primary support.

It's easy to blame Kim Beazley for what happened in 2001. His advisers and senior parliamentarians must share some of that blame. But the only point in being wise after the event is if it ensures the same mistakes are not repeated.

What sort of electorate produced the so-called "no change" result of November 2001? Far from being "relaxed and comfortable", it seems to have been tense and discomforted. Qualitative research from a number of sources paints a picture of a society worried about change and often powerless in its attempts to cope with it. Optimism about social progress is thin on the ground. People no longer believe their children will be better off than they are. Society is seen as less generous, less relaxed, and there is the feeling that people are more concerned with themselves, less interested in the outside world. Work and family life are increasingly out of harmony with each other. The social commentator Hugh Mackay puts it this way: "The struggle to balance work and family is becoming a bigger challenge for Australians as the pressures of work grow more intense, the rate of family breakdown increases and a sense of stress grows more pervasive."

If this is even half–right, it goes some way towards explaining the hardening of community attitudes towards the unemployed, the Aborigines and perhaps the asylum seekers. Thanks in large part to Pauline Hanson, even Australia's traditional egalitarianism has been given a new twist: everyone should be treated equally regardless of need.

These are perceptions, recordings of inchoate feelings. The underlying reality for low-income families is more disturbing. Last year Professors Bob Gregory, Jeff Borland and Peter Sheehan published the results of a three-year research project entitled *Work Rich, Work Poor* that examined changes in the labour market in the 1990s and their consequences. They concluded that these changes had "generat[ed] deepening division within Australia".

It's not a surprising finding. Apart from documenting the decline in full-time jobs and a dramatic rise in casual and part-time employment, the study also drew attention to the "massive increase in demand" on social security:

> For example, by 1997–98, 20 per cent of all income units with a head of working age were dependent on social security as their principal source of income, by comparison with less than 3 per cent in 1970. By June 1999, 17.4 per cent of all dependent children were being brought up in jobless families.

This sort of analysis points up the vacuity of parliamentary slanging matches about how many jobs were created when, about unemployment now and then, about which party happened to preside over the fastest growth rate.

But surely most Australians are getting richer? As the authors of *Work Rich, Work Poor* point out:

> To those who focus on aggregate economic indicators, talk of a social crisis, especially one driven by the trends within the economy, is incomprehensible. After all, for much of the past decade

> employment and average real earnings have been growing strongly, and unemployment has been falling.

The Coalition has dilated extensively about the new jobs it has created, but what is the nature of these new jobs? Of 527,000 jobs created between 1998 and 2001, 462,000 pay less than the average wage, only 72,000 pay more. Middle-income jobs (between $700 and $1400 per week) increased by fewer than 1000.

It is this social crisis of widespread insecurity, coupled with a growing gap between the affluence of the many and the 20 per cent locked into the web of social security, that Labor has to address if it is to be taken seriously as a party that speaks for the disadvantaged.

Language is part of the problem and it creates distrust in the political process. Contemporary politicians talk in the jargon of their trade. At present, this is usually the jargon of economists, which conveys little to the average person. What, for example, does the expression "underlying rate of inflation" mean to most people? The best communicators in Australian politics, including Neville Wran, Don Dunstan and Mick Young, never used jargon. Joh Bjelke-Petersen and his wife Flo were also effective political communicators, strange as it may seem, given their tendency to muddled language. Joh used to call a press conference "feeding the chooks".

When politicians talk of jobs created and earnings going up, most lower paid workers (not to mention those out of work) can't relate these claims to their own experience. The language of conventional politics is equally hopeless in addressing the stress placed on families by the increased number of women of child-bearing age in the workforce, by the longer hours worked by people in full-time jobs and the higher costs of child care for low-income families.

With this picture of dissatisfaction among the voters, what image do voters have of politicians? Well, in a poll conducted by Irving Saulwick and Associates in August last year, 37 per cent of those interviewed thought that today's politicians showed poorer qualities of leadership than those of previous generations, 53 per cent thought they were about the same and 10 per cent thought they showed better qualities of leadership. Politicians have rarely been particularly popular and we have no idea what the 53 per cent actually think. They may be fatalists, they may think politicians are just as bad as they always were.

Yet even these stark figures are misleading. Most people don't spend too much time thinking about politics. They think instead about things like their jobs, their families and sport. Politics touches their lives at the margin. Young people, in particular, show little interest in political parties, except for the Greens who are seen as more "principled" and more likely to tell it like it is. The Democrats are regarded with an ambivalence that matches their ambivalence about themselves. The most hopeful thing is that people still value the act of putting their ballot paper in the box.

The most profoundly disillusioning event in 2001 for those who believed in a humanitarian and compassionate Labor Party was its response to the *Tampa* incident and the engineered refugee crisis. People searched in vain for a sign of difference between the ALP and the Coalition. On 19 October it became clear there was none. On that day some 350 asylum seekers were drowned when an overcrowded Indonesian fishing vessel sank off the coast of Java. The husband of one survivor, a woman whose three young children had drowned, was living in Australia on a temporary protection visa. The Immigration Minister, Philip Ruddock, refused to waive the conditions of the visa, effectively preventing the husband from visiting his wife in Indonesia. This was an inhumane and cruel decision, and Kim Beazley acquiesced in it.

The Labor leadership had overlooked the fact that the potentially explosive issue of "boat people" had been on the public agenda since early in the year. As a result they were left stunned and flat-footed. No alternative was suggested. It didn't seem to matter that the platform of the party, updated at the National Conference in August 2001, contained a clear and compassionate statement of principle in relation to asylum seekers and refugees. Apart from forcefully articulated criticism from Tasmanian Green Senator Bob Brown and from Peter Andren, the Independent member for Calare, and rather less forceful criticism from the Democrats, there was no political opposition to the government's stance. Within the Parliamentary Labor Party and the shadow ministry, some were profoundly dismayed at the position adopted by the leadership group. They conveyed this privately to friends but stuck by the party line, which is almost inevitable in the course of an election campaign. Some of them, like Duncan Kerr and Carmen Lawrence, spoke about their concerns after the election.

Opinion polls, which recorded overwhelming support for Howard's stance on "Border Protection", led to widespread introspection among liberal-minded Australians about what sort of country Australia had become. Was this the same country that had shown a benign, tolerant face to the world at the 2000 Sydney Olympics? That boasted about the success of its migrant programs and multiculturalism? Had we become selfish, xenophobic, racist? There was soul searching, there was confusion and fear; and fear, as Arthur Calwell once explained to me, is "the most potent weapon in politics".

What happened was more complex than racism or xenophobia. Two weeks before the election I talked about the refugees with the One Nation candidate for a Queensland rural electorate. At first he was assertive, almost belligerent. "Don't you try and tell me those Muslims coming here in boats aren't terrorists," he said, an idea planted in his mind by a headline-grabbing remark of Defence Minister Peter Reith. When he'd calmed down, I asked him his views about immigration generally. After a few seconds silence, he said, "Well, we can't be a selfish nation. We're basically a Christian country. We've got to have migrants, preferably from Europe." I asked him about Asian migration. "Asians," he said, "Well, I've never met a bad one yet. Good reliable people. Hard workers. Yes, I like Asians, except what I see in Cabramatta. But these Muslims can't even get on with each other." Can this man from Pauline Hanson's party be called a "racist"? I think not. Confused, and susceptible to the blandishments of threat experts? I think so.

The ALP was caught in the headlights, frozen between the sentiment of the national platform and belief in compassionate, humane values on the one hand and opinion polls on the other. Labor's confusion was ruthlessly exploited by Howard and his henchmen Reith, Costello and Ruddock. Howard played two cards, one of which seemed suspiciously like racism, the other involving a spurious appeal to a bus-stop egalitarianism. This second card said: these people are not victims but selfish "queue jumpers" unprepared to wait for entry to the promised land. Australians, sometimes uncertain about their own motives, were provided with an alibi: I'm not a racist, just a fervent believer in queues.

Do we have to hang our heads in shame as racists or have we, as members of a society built on successive waves of immigration, suddenly become peculiarly sensitive to what some right-wing politicians and commentators call "cultural difference"? Is the current climate only a border protection issue or is there something here among us, something new to be worried about?

The writer Gitta Sereny, who has devoted a lifetime to exploring the underlying causes of racism, sheds some light on this question:

> In any discussion of the problems in our world today, racism must rank high. Not because we are soft-minded liberals obsessed with countless crimes throughout history induced by colour, religion, tribalism or chauvinism of one kind or another. But because the poison which we hoped and believed had been eradicated in our own time by the knowledge of the ultimate evil – the gas chamber murders committed by the Nazis – is in fact still present, not in any one area of discrimination or racism, or in a restricted number of specific rulers or governments, but in all humankind. I call it "Inner Racism".

This is an unpalatable view but it is also comforting to think that Australians are no different from anyone else. Circumstances of isolation, perceived threats and a relatively small population perhaps produce our own special brand of the disease. The more important question is how a society behaves when confronted with a problem that touches its innermost fears. With tolerance? With the will to do unto others as we, in similar circumstances, would have them do unto us?

On these issues Labor was silent. The commentators, the pollsters and the pundits may be right to say that if the ALP had opposed the government on the *Tampa* incident and its aftermath, or even suggested an alternative, it would have lost the election by a bigger margin. But this is speculation because the ALP did none of these things. Beyond speculation, however, is the knowledge that Australia would have been less diminished in the eyes of the world, the ALP more respected in the minds of deeply concerned voters, and the Coalition isolated in its own grubby opportunism.

And sometimes courageous political stands produce lasting or long-term dividends. There are examples of this in the history of the ALP, opposition to the Vietnam War being the most obvious. In the election of 1966 the ALP was soundly defeated on this issue. By 1972 this stand on principle had become part of Labor's historic achievement. In 2001 Labor was again faced with its classic dilemma. In May, at the centenary celebrations dinner, Kim Beazley put it this way: "Winning government must always be our highest priority, not winning at any cost, but winning so that we can better the conditions of our core supporters and improve this country's future." Beazley's statement goes to the heart of the party.

It's worth remembering that the ALP has always done best in federal elections when it has set the political agenda, when it has involved its members as agents of change and enthused a wider section of the community with a sense of excitement and vision. A small target strategy does none of these things. It is contrary to ALP sentiment and tradition, demoralising to the membership and boring for the electorate. And if it fails, it fails devastatingly. As one shadow minister put it after the election, "The problem with being a small target is that if you're hit, you're buggered."

It was, as the London *Sun* once wrote of the Queen in her *annus horribilis*, a bum year. It was Labor's year of grave misjudgements, of failure to project any alternative vision which could capture the imagination of voters, a year in which the morale among the rank and file progressively declined. Morale was so poor not just because of the absence of a credible political agenda, but because members felt they belonged to an organisation that could not provide a climate for political ideas or political action. Worst of all, members of the Labor Party wondered whether they had become irrelevant. And whether the Labor Party, in turn, had ceased to be relevant to the politics of the nation.

CRASHING THE PARTY

In April 2002 a subterranean dispute within the ALP surfaced in the media. The correspondent of the Melbourne *Age* described it as a "bitter internal power struggle". The Health Services Union threatened disaffiliation from the ALP, alleging that senior party officials had been interfering in its affairs. The press reported suggestions of money changing hands (subsequently denied) and threats of legal action. The ALP officials involved were the National President, Greg Sword, and the Victorian State Secretary, David Feeney. Both belong to the Right faction; both wanted control of the Health Services Union. On 12 April the dispute inside the union ended up in the Federal Court with the state secretary of the union seeking access to documents relating to union finances. In May the argument spilt over to the Victorian state conference. In June Sword's union, the National Union of Workers, withdrew from the Right faction.

What is this dispute about? It's not a struggle over ideas, or a battle between the left and right of the party, whatever that means today. It's an internal dispute in the right-wing faction of the ALP. Control of the union, the *Age* reported, will ensure the victor "power over a bloc of votes at the ALP's state conference and greater influence on party pre-selection panels".

These disputes happen all too often. Newspapers report them in mysterious articles that are almost impossible to decipher. The public is probably baffled and bored. To the average person the struggle probably looks like a brawl in a pub that threatens to spill out onto the street; best to walk past without making eye contact with any of the participants.

But these disputes represent something important. They are signs of a Labor Party corrupted by petty conflicts, dominated by what unionist Martin Foley calls factional "warlords", and distracted from its historic purpose. This is the new inward-looking, corrosive culture of the ALP.

Of course, factional disputes are hardly unknown to the Labor Party. What is new is the domination of the party hierarchy by a new class of labour movement professionals who rely on factions and unions affiliated to the party for their career advancement. These people come from the ranks of political advisers, trade union policy officers and electoral office staff. Individually they can be thoughtful and decent people. Collectively they are destroying the diversity and appeal of the ALP and its affiliated unions.

The overall effect on the ALP has been profoundly destructive. Federally, the party is in retreat. Its primary votes, its membership and the breadth of people it sends to parliament are all shrinking. These things are intimately connected, and they are made possible by a party structure that has barely changed in the past century, that is moribund and out of touch with contemporary society.

The membership of Australian political parties has never been large. But in 2002 Labor's membership is lower (relative to the population) than at any time since the party became a major political force. With no comprehensive national database, a figure of 50,000 is a reasonable estimate of total membership, even including the large number of members signed up at concessional rates in branch-stacking campaigns. This, as South Australian Senator Chris Schacht has poignantly observed, is about the same as the membership of the Adelaide Football Club. It is a woeful figure.

A second area of shrinkage is in the occupational backgrounds of members of the Parliamentary Labor Party. In 1978, the year after Gough Whitlam left politics, the parliamentary party of sixty-four members contained ten former union officials, six of whom had worked in the trade or calling represented by their unions, six from wholesale and retail business and two accountants. It also included three farmers, six lawyers, three academics, four medical practitioners, two policemen, five public servants, five tradesmen and five teachers. There was one engineer, one journalist, one former merchant marine officer and one shearer, the late Mick Young. Five were former members of state parliaments and two former party officials. It was a pretty good social mix and something that Gough Whitlam had vigorously pursued.

The mix was still there in the first Hawke ministry, which had among its members former farmers, businessmen, academics, lawyers and union officials, as well as a former engine driver, a teacher, a retailer, a waterside worker and a shearer. The government that reformed and deregulated the economy was not made up of political mandarins.

Yet look at what a cloistered profession the Parliamentary Labor Party has become. After Kim Beazley's vigorous campaign in the 1998 election, Labor returned to parliament with a party of ninety-six members of vastly changed occupational backgrounds. Although one medical practitioner, one public servant and one engineer remained, no farmers or tradesmen did. There were two academics and two teachers, as well as nine lawyers, but the whole social complexion had changed.

What had replaced a broad spectrum of backgrounds was a new class of political operator who had been filtered through the net of ALP machine politics. Out of a total of ninety-six members, fifty-three came from jobs in party or union offices. These members described themselves variously as "administrators", "officials" and "electoral officers". There were also ten former members of state parliaments and nine described as political consultants, advisers and lobbyists.

Seventy-six of the ninety-six members had tertiary qualifications; a mere two had trade qualifications. Labor's politicians have nearly all been to factional finishing school but not many have been to the school of hard knocks. The ALP has become truly professional, and, in the process of professionalising itself, has lost much of its capacity to relate to the broader community and a lot of its charm.

The narrowing parliamentary base is symbolised by the predominance of a number of holy families of Labor politics. Once upon a time it was conservative clans like the Downers and Anthonys who tended to monopolise parliamentary dynasties, but today the ALP has a rival list that reads like a row of gentlemen's outfitters in the lower end of Bond Street: Beazley and Son, Crean and Son, Ferguson Brothers, Fitzgibbon and Son, Brown and Hoare (father and daughter), McLelland and Son ... The list goes on and they are all worthy and respectable concerns; there can be no serious objection to their continuing in the family business. Between them, however, the present generation of dynastic representatives makes up about 10 per cent of the ALP lower house.

Following parental career paths is not unusual in professions such as law, medicine and dentistry, but in politics it is. The trend points to the absence of a truly competitive selection process in which community stature and talent carry more votes than history and sentiment.

The Labor Party used to claim that its trade union links meant that it had a wider socio-economic and occupational representation in parliament than the conservative parties, "with their almost exclusively middle-class image". Well, time has modified old truths. Labor has more members with university degrees than ever before, and while tertiary qualifications in the general workforce are usually seen as a good thing, in politics it may not necessarily be so. A common touch can be more important: a politician's ability to relate to voters and voters' capacity to relate to politicians is sometimes helped by the knowledge and the belief that they have shared common experiences; that they speak the same language. Remoteness is an enemy of communication. The late Mick Young, one of the best and shrewdest political communicators of the 1970s and 1980s, was an outstanding example of a politician who never lost touch with the voting public. He had wit and spoke a language that everyone could understand.

In July 1999 Kim Beazley announced an initiative to attract young voters to Labor. Beazley called on "the infusion of new talent that arrived at last year's election to hit the streets and tell the young what the ALP is all about". This was always going to be a tough call. Of the eight new MPs in the talent team (ranging in age from twenty-six to thirty-seven) five had made their way into politics through union offices. The remaining three had worked as electorate officers for members of parliament. Among the eight there is clearly ability. All are university graduates, most have valuable local political experience working in demanding electorates, three are now shadow ministers and three are parliamentary secretaries to shadow ministers. But competence of this sort doesn't necessarily in help in selling the message to the young, as the election results demonstrate. Nicola Roxon, one of the eight and now a shadow minister, noted recently that Labor's primary vote among 18–24 year olds had fallen by fourteen percentage points between the 1984 and 2001 federal elections.

There are other alarming signs. The Federal ALP has retreated from the bush. On the Australian mainland it holds only three predominantly rural seats, and each is represented by an MP strongly identified with the local community. Seats such as Kalgoorlie in Western Australia and Grey in South Australia, once safe Labor seats, now look safe Coalition. The electoral map is littered with the names of regional seats that were once held by the ALP, often for long periods, including five in New South Wales and four in Queensland.

In the 1990s the ALP gained nothing from dissatisfaction with the National Party and the decline in its parliamentary representation, and this is largely a result of neglect. In 2001 Kim Beazley wrote that at election time Chifley had told his father to "Watch the wheat seats." Beazley went on: "Now I can say to my daughters on election night, 'Watch the regions.'" At the last election his daughters wouldn't have had much joy. Over several years Labor had failed to develop a strategy to accommodate the particular circumstances of regional Australia and offered little support for the party branches or candidates in rural seats.

In the Queensland rural seat of Kennedy, held by Labor for sixty-four of the last one hundred years, I talked in October 2001 with the ALP candidate Alan Neilan. He lived at Normanton on the Gulf of Carpentaria, and between January 2001 and the election in November he drove 30,000 kilometres in his own car, visiting small towns and outback stations in this vast rural electorate. He received no financial support from federal ALP election funds. Local branches, he told me, "kicked in" to help him pay for petrol and leaflets. I asked him why he did it. He said something about the need for a better understanding of the sort of outback communities in which he works and lives.

Perhaps he dreamt of explaining that in Canberra. But he had no hope of winning and he knew it. The former National Party member and independent candidate Bob Katter had it in the bag. Kennedy is Katter country. But Neilan finished second, beating the National Party candidate. He got no help because Kennedy was not a "targeted seat". Plenty of other rural and regional seats are not targeted by the ALP; the candidates and the local branches have to do it on their own.

If the ALP hopes to govern for all Australians, then it has to bridge the divide between the cities and non-metropolitan Australia. This requires some understanding of "rural values". For many urban dwellers these can seem conservative, but that's only half right. More than in the cities, the values of egalitarianism, community and mateship remain strong in rural Australia. It is ironic, then, that the Labor Party, which makes much of its egalitarian ideals, is so often seen as bureaucratic, too close to the trade unions and just plain uninterested. The Bracks government in Victoria, elected in 1999 on the rural vote, shows how the attitudinal gulf between metropolitan and non-metropolitan Australia can be overcome.

Labor's "heartland", its historically working-class vote in the city and suburbs, is also contracting. In 2001, the ALP lost the heartland seat of Dobell in NSW and one marginal seat. In other cities, too, it failed to win seats that it might have expected to win based on traditional loyalties. But people can get too hung up on the idea of a heartland. As the percentage of swinging voters rises and the past pattern of committed voting for political parties declines, the idea becomes less valid. A narrow focus on policies designed to regain former heartlands will not return an ALP government. Only a party that had lost sight of the rest of Australia could think that it will.

Factions

Three years ago I had a phone call from an active faction leader asking me to vote for him in a pre-selection ballot. Such phone calls are part of the nitty-gritty of politics. All of us who have been in politics have had moments when we have had to count numbers, phone people up and ask them for a vote. I asked the caller a question: "I know your reputation as an organiser for your faction but what do you believe you can contribute to parliament?" There was a long pause. Then he said, and I quote, "Well, I'll be able to organise the Left better in parliament."

Labor's founders saw parliament as a means of advancing the objectives of the Labor Party and the interests of working people. This bloke looks no further than the interests of his faction. He is not alone. He belongs to a narrow category of ALP members: the aspirational politician.

Factions are destroying the quality of Labor's MPs. Factions stack branches and manipulate trade unions. Both branch-stacking and interference in trade union affairs are against party rules but the national rule against factional branch-stacking doesn't work because the factions don't support it. No penalties have been imposed by internal party disciplinary bodies. In 1999 a South Australian member of parliament, Ralph Clarke, went to the Supreme Court to force his state executive to reverse a sudden and unusual increase in party membership in Clarke's electorate. Clarke was successful but only after going to an outside court: the party had no effective mechanism for resolving such a dispute. The court judgement reflected badly on the ALP: in essence the judge said that an important Australian institution was being damaged by improper practices.

In 1963, in response to interference in trade union affairs by Industrial Groups linked to the old DLP, the National Conference adopted a resolution that deplored "interference in trade unions' activities by any government, outside individuals or organisations". Today the interference in a number of affiliated unions comes not from outside but from factions within the ALP – interference that was once anathema to the trade union movement. The 1963 resolution remains in force but, as with branch-stacking, factions ensure it is not acted upon.

Factional interference in trade union elections operates quite simply. Factional leaders intervene to get their man or woman into a key position in the union. Success is followed by payback: the union, under its factional management, delivers bloc votes at state ALP conferences, strengthening the faction's position in ballots for internal party positions and in pre-selections for parliamentary seats. A union controlled by a faction is able to provide staff jobs to aspirants for parliamentary selection. It is a closed and sometimes vicious circle, which distracts unions from their true role, bleeding their energy and efficiency as representatives of their members.

Unions, of course, have had a long involvement in politics. They started the ALP and once dominated party conferences with numbers and ideas. They pumped their best-qualified members into parliament, often from self-educated and politically motivated rank and file members. Now it is the other way round. ALP factions try to capture the allegiance of unions to advance the interests of a breed of Labor professionals. These professionals do not come from the rank and file of union members, and so a gap widens between the leadership of the union and its members. Too often the members switch off politics as a result, to the long-term detriment of the ALP.

ALP members spend a fair amount of time talking about factions. The talk is not so much about what factions believe in or stand for; there is not much evidence that they believe in or stand for anything. The talk relates more to who is going to win which ballot and why. Today's factions are about arithmetic not philosophy. At best the factional warlords are masters of backroom compromises. At worst they are proof that even on the narrow stage of limited ambitions, power corrupts.

In 1999 I had a coffee with the Victorian senator Robert Ray. The former minister Graham Richardson, who knows more than a little about these matters, once described Ray as "one of the best factional operators the party has ever seen or ever will see". Our coffee came in the middle of a particularly bitter, though looking back on it entirely Byzantine, factional feud. Confused, I asked Ray what the ideological differences between Labor's "Left" and "Right" factions were these days. "There are none", Ray replied in a fit of candour. "It's purely tribal."

Tribalism has much to be said for it. It promotes loyalty, solidarity, efficiency. However, it's also primitive, anti-intellectual and leads to fiefdoms concerned with territory rather than ideas. Why, when ideological differences are no longer important, do people still join factions in the ALP? Belonging to a group (or tribe) is comforting in the insecure environment of politics. More importantly, being a faction member is seen as the road to political advancement in the party hierarchy or into parliament. The rewards are more for loyalty to the group than any particular ability, and sometimes the promises of factional leaders are not honoured.

Factions also inflict collateral damage on the party. In June the women's ginger group Emily's List, which has campaigned with some success to increase the number of ALP women in parliament, warned that the ALP would remain in the wilderness unless it broke "the stranglehold of male factional bosses". This echoes the opinion of Labor's first woman federal cabinet minister, Susan Ryan, who argues that the special contribution which women have to make to parliament has been subordinated to factional allegiances. Emily's List identified issues such as maternity leave and equal pay as requiring attention if Labor is to win government. There are many more.

From time to time most political parties divide into factions of one kind or another. These coalesce around a set of ideas or attitudes or in support of a candidate or group of candidates for internal party positions. Often enough they disband when the issue that brought them together is resolved and they no longer have a function. Not in the ALP. Here they are entrenched, part of the landscape and the culture.

The history of modern factions centres on New South Wales and Victoria. In New South Wales the Right has been the dominant faction. In Victoria the Left (or non-Right) was most influential in the '70s and '80s (though not any longer).

In some respects this is a tale of two cities. Cultural differences between the two states have influenced the style and substance of Labor's factions.

In Victoria the political culture has a lot to do with Melbourne University and the strength of its student political clubs in the three decades following World War II. These clubs produced a number of left intellectuals whose writings influenced Labor thinking, including Manning Clark, Ian Turner, Noel Ebbels, Stephen Murray-Smith, Geoff Serle, Alan Davies and Jim Cairns. Some became ALP activists after leaving the Communist Party in the 1960s. Others followed the British intellectual tradition exemplified in the writings of R.H. Tawney and G.D.H. Cole. Their influences were predominantly British and Fabian, and certainly more European than American.

In the New South Wales Right, where pragmatism and success go hand in hand, American politics has had more influence. The knowledge of American politics among a number of leaders of the NSW Right is something of a cultural phenomenon. They know how Chicago's Mayor Daley manipulated Democratic Party conventions, they understand presidential primaries, they've read the biographies of Truman and the Kennedys and Lyndon Johnson. Their major concession to British politics is the habit of calling Liberals "Tories", a practice not followed in Victoria. While the Victorians messed about with ideas, they were into practical, hard-nosed politics. While the Victorians enjoyed a vaguely Marxist and European socialist belief in the perfectibility of man, the NSW Right was the home of the ALP's true Darwinians.

There are sensible historical reasons why these divisions exist. On three occasions during the twentieth century the Labor Party lost government at the federal level because of splits over ideological issues. In 1916 there was the split over conscription, in 1931 over the economic response to the Great Depression, and in 1955 over attitudes to communism. The divisions spilt over into the party membership. In the Parliamentary Labor Party the arguments were resolved by one side leaving. In 1955 some affiliated unions and a big section of the party membership left as well.

These experiences profoundly wounded Labor's psyche. If the protagonists of contemporary factionalism are to be believed, the underlying reason for their existence is to prevent splits, manage conflict behind closed doors and present an impression of a happy unified party to the public. In a sense this works. A public largely uninterested in politics and cynical about politicians is not too curious about the internal machinations of political parties. The façade is what they see.

If outsiders wanted to look behind the façade, what would they make of "Right", "Labour Unity", "Non-aligned", "Left", "Socialist Left", "Broad Left", "Centre Left", "Centre Unity", "Pledge Left"? These are some names of factions that in recent years have come and gone and sometimes remained, as faction leaders grapple with the task of encapsulating in a brand name the nuances of their supposed ideological allegiance. The fact that most of these names are irrelevant to contemporary politics, that they are fixed in history rather than reality, doesn't seem to matter. It is all somewhat reminiscent of the fragmented "Peoples' Liberation Front of Judea" in the Monty Python film *Life of Brian*.

Labor's factionalism hardened in the early 1980s with the development of a National Right faction. According to Graham Richardson, who had a lot to do with this, the National Right had two aims: to get Bob Hawke elected as Labor leader and "to form a loose amalgam of these disparate groups" identified as "anti-Left". In themselves these were unexceptional ambitions. But inevitably they led to a reaction from the Left and the spread of factionalism from New South Wales and Victoria into other states and territories.

In 1984 the Centre Left was formed in Canberra. Bill Hayden saw the new faction as "a powerhouse of ideas … guided by principles of equity and progressive distribution". Barry Jones was less sanguine: the Centre Left was "a political lonely-hearts club. What draws us together is that no one else loves us." Certainly, by the late '80s the Centre Left was the only grouping that claimed ideas as its raison d'être. The others were too busy organising numbers and dividing the spoils.

One of the great strengths of the Hawke government was the breadth of factional representation, which gave stability to the parliamentary party.

True Believers, the history of Labor mentioned earlier, states that, "A December 1984 count put the Right at 45, the Left 34, the Centre Left 27, with 5 Victorian independents who had links to a greater or lesser degree with the Centre Left. This left just seven members non-aligned." The Centre Left grouping provided a disproportionately large number of ministers; they went straight into the ministry on merit, having been active Opposition front-benchers prior to the election in 1983. The Right and Left resented this and gradually asserted claims to ministerial positions on the basis of faction numbers, rather than talent. As a result, by the time Paul Keating became leader, the quality of the ministry had declined. Today the Centre Left still exists, although it is greatly diminished in numbers and influence.

In the 1990s, as major factions honed their organisational skills, it became harder to tell just what they were organising for. Once there had been genuine differences and real debates. But what was "Left" and what was "Right" in the last decade of the twentieth century? If the factional leaders of the 1980s were the sorcerers, their apprentices have further refined the art. A touch of evil has been added to the fascination. It is difficult to imagine that the sorcerers, people like Robert Ray and Gerry Hand, understood what they were creating or what would happen when ideological differences disappeared.

In 1988 Bob McMullan, then the ALP's general secretary, warned that in the longer term factionalism "contains the seeds of our destruction ... we can't go on like this or we will become ossified." McMullan has maintained his independence from factions. He might have advanced faster, even to the deputy leadership, if he hadn't. After the 2001 Elections the leadership positions were decided by a straight Left/Right factional deal to install Simon Crean and Jenny Macklin, without any vote of the parliamentary party. This is unprecedented in the recent history of the ALP.

Can the ALP, to use McMullan's words, "go on like this"? Yes, but only downhill. Factional allegiances and deals lead to mediocrity. A senior shadow minister described the Federal Parliamentary Labor Party to me in September last year as "bland, fair-average quality and occupying a grey middle ground". There are, he said "no stand-outs here".

This may seem unduly harsh – the shadow cabinet contains some talent (though, he's right, no obvious future leaders). But how can "stand-out" candidates for parliament emerge when federal electorates are designated as "belonging" to the Right or the Left? When potential candidates are vetted by factional leaders with a vested interest in mediocrity? When, in return for factional support, successful candidates are asked, among other things, to provide places on their parliamentary staff for aspiring factional apparatchiks? What sort of people who are successful in their careers or communities, and who might be good candidates, are likely to be bothered with all that? Sadly not many, so the "gene pool" of quality, experience and interest declines.

Factionalism also contributes to the party's shrinking membership and to the deterioration in its quality. "Branch-stacking" for purposes of voting in ballots might for short periods increase the numbers in certain branches but members recruited in this way are rarely committed or involved.

Within the factions the ossification is intellectual. Not all factional leaders are by nature sympathetic to radical ideas or to an atmosphere of free discussion. By inclination they are usually control freaks devoted to manipulation rather than thought. They're rarely a joy to be with over a good lunch and they tend to talk about one subject, without much humour. Those who make it through the system to parliamentary positions seldom have much impact. As public figures they're about as attractive as Hannibal Lecter. They develop considerable political skills (useful in tribal conflict) in the distribution of propaganda, the enrolment of voters, spotting trends in polling and the counting of votes. These are important skills but essentially restricted, concentrating too much on narrow goals.

Some psychologists divide leaders into two groups: "transactional leaders" and "transforming leaders". Factionalism produces "transactional" leaders skilled at negotiating across a table but far fewer "transforming" leaders focused on defeating conservatives and winning government. With some notable exceptions such as current senators Robert Ray (Right) and John Faulkner (Left), they have not produced many members of parliament who can speak "off the cuff", who know how to have a go at the conservative side of politics. Nor do they provide many leaders who engage in critical analysis based on a framework of ideas about Australian society and its future. Hyped-up by the heady tribalism of group loyalty, factional warriors are prone to suffer, like athletes overdosed on steroids, from testicular atrophy when confronted by the real enemy. They can make good constituent members, but in parliament their identity is swamped by sectional fealty and the need for tribal approval. Because of this a curious phenomenon occurs: they often have no strongly developed sense of difference from the Liberals sitting opposite them.

Factions are not going to disappear overnight. Nearly every federal ALP member of parliament relies on factional support or on factional cross-deals. To change the culture of factions requires much goodwill and a more outward-looking culture. It means allowing Labor to imagine a future for itself and to build a broader membership base in which there is the opportunity for a hundred flowers to bloom.

Unions

Whenever the question of restructuring the ALP arises, the limelight falls on the relationship between the unions and the party. Should the unions have almost all the delegates to a state conference as they once did? Or should it be 60 per cent as it is now, or perhaps 50 per cent, or less? These possible adjustments seem more about appearance than reality. Martin Foley of the Australian Services Union asked the most germane question in his submission to the current Hawke–Wran inquiry into the state of the ALP: "Why – beyond serving the careerist interests of an elite of labour movement professionals – do unions affiliate to the ALP at all in the modern Australian context? What is in it for the unions? What is in it for the ALP?"

The union–ALP relationship has degenerated into a bad habit. It damages the ALP. It damages the unions even more. It may be time for the formal relationship to end: to have a friendly divorce.

A review of the Labor Party observed that:

> The issue of the traditional links between the ALP and the trade unions constitutes a problem of considerable magnitude, and is seen … as critical to the future of the party … These links have remained formally little altered over time, despite the shift from a provincial to a national society, the revolution in communications, the great changes in the nature and the composition of the workforce, and the transformation of the trade union movement itself. Yet the unions affiliated with the ALP today are basically the same as those affiliated in the first decade of the century, and the form of affiliation remains state-based.

That review took place in 1978, nearly a quarter of a century ago. Little had changed for a long time before then; little if anything has changed since.

The argument usually advanced against formal union affiliation to the party is that it has on occasions embarrassed the ALP; it is outmoded, a relic of a bygone age. That's no longer the most important issue. In 2002 the real issue is manipulation of power within the party and the effect this has on party membership and the free development of ideas.

The case for a relationship with the unions is largely based on history and sentiment. But another aspect is often overlooked: the claim that union influence ensures that the ALP "keeps its feet on the ground" with regard to social policy and living standards. Over the years this has been true, but union affiliation is not necessary for this to occur.

The most obvious recent example of a successful relationship between unions and government was during the period of the Hawke and Keating governments. The Wages Accord, directly negotiated between the government and the ACTU, provided wage stability and a forum for dialogue, without which the wide-ranging economic reforms of the 1980s could not have been achieved. The Accord also enabled the government to draw on the talents of union leaders who, particularly in manufacturing, frequently understood the requirements of modern industry better than the manufacturers themselves.

In hindsight there has been some criticism of the Accord. Some union officials argue that the government got more out of it than the unions; that, in the words of ACTU Secretary, Greg Combet, it caused union leaders "to take our eye off the ball" and distracted them from recruiting new members and organising new industries. Others, on the left and right of the union movement, agree. The experiment, although it brought important gains, is unlikely to be repeated in a similar form.

In 2002 things have moved on. What the ALP and the union movement have most in common now is a membership steadily declining, and for similar reasons. Both have been slow to adapt to changing social circumstances; both share, in various degrees, an aversion to democratic member participation; both have hierarchies often seen as out of touch. The ALP and the unions are like two old mates waiting at a bus stop on shaky legs, leaning on each other for support, reminiscing about the past and hoping something will turn up; a bus, an ambulance or someone like Bob Hawke.

At least the ACTU has realised this. Its "Unions at Work" strategy is designed to make unions more democratic, to promote social change and to improve communication with its own members and with the public. The ALP has no such strategy.

The question is not whether there should be a relationship but what sort of relationship it should be. History suggests it should be about shared values and ideas, and policies that reflect mutual interests. So long as it is mainly about control of a small pond, the relationship is not of much real value to either partner.

The usual argument for changing the 60–40 rule is that the decline of union membership has been so dramatic that unions no longer represent either a majority or a broad spectrum of Australian workers. In August

2001 unions made up less than 25 per cent of the total workforce and only 19.2 per cent of the private sector workforce. (Compare this to 1978 when union membership made up 57 per cent of the workforce.) Unions affiliated with the ALP represent less than 15 per cent of the workforce. Why, the argument goes, should unions have the numbers in party conferences when they no longer have the numbers in the wider world?

The past twenty-five years have seen no new union affiliations to the ALP in technical and professional areas. Membership of unions in the growth sectors of the economy – information technology, telecommunications, electronics, biotechnology and financial and business services – is low, sometimes tiny. Jobs in these industries are often occupied by skilled younger workers used to moving from one job to another, many of whom prefer contract employment to award coverage. They work in jobs where demand for skilled labour usually exceeds supply; their salaries and conditions are such that they see no need for union membership.

Unions have also been sidelined by the huge growth in services provided by contractors, ranging from lawn-mowing and house-cleaning to highly skilled technical assistance. Where once the consumer would call a large company or government business for help, today he or she calls a small business or individual who may work from home. To these workers, well-paid or not, unions are irrelevant. In general, service workers are hard to organise, especially those in casual and part-time positions. Just one in five part-time employees is a member of a union.

Social change has put enormous pressure on trade unions, and there is no point in their turning to the political party with which some of them are affiliated for help. The ALP can't turn the clock back any more than they can. It would be silly to try.

There are other unpalatable facts. At the best of times an estimated 40 per cent of unionists vote for political parties other than the ALP. Individual membership of unionists in the ALP is low and has been for many years, which simply suggests that unionists have no greater interest in politics than anyone else. A number of unions struggle to find enough ALP members in their ranks to fill their delegate entitlement at state conferences. In such cases delegations are made up of various non-members chosen by the union secretary. (In the mid-1960s the author attended Victorian state conferences as a plasterer, a pastry cook and a bricklayer. He was not proficient in any of these trades.)

The tensions associated with union affiliation were well illustrated in March 2002 with the resignation from the ALP of the Victorian Secretary of the Electrical Trades Union, Dean Mighell, and the Secretary of the United Firefighters Union, Peter Marshall. Mighell belongs to the Left and has a reputation as an industrial militant. He's intelligent and drives a hard bargain with employers, which is, after all, what union officials are supposed to do. He's not, one suspects, easily duchessed. Mighell complains, with some justification, that the ALP has lost its way. He was quoted as saying that, "If unions really were dominant the ALP would be a very different party."

The difficulty with this view is threefold. First, the union movement is not politically homogeneous. There are right-wing, moderate and left-wing unions, and unions controlled by officials who have little interest in politics at all. If unions had 100 per cent of ALP conference delegates and even more union officials in parliament there is no reason to believe that Mighell's political views would have more influence than they do now.

Second, Mighell's argument ignores the fact that some powerful unions are controlled not by officials "off the job" but by middle-class mercenaries who see the union movement as a pathway to a political career. These are the people who are best suited by the affiliated union structure, who live and breathe in the vicious circle of faction and union described earlier.

Third, the disenchantment with the ALP is a tacit admission of the failure of the present system of affiliation. All those former union advisers and research officers "bumped into parliament" by the present system, plus a number of former union officials and three former ACTU presidents in safe seats in federal parliament – Simon Crean, Martin Ferguson and Jenny George – don't seem to be delivering the goods.

For the union movement this is surely the vital point. What benefits does affiliation to the Labor Party give to their membership? In his submission to the Hawke–Wran inquiry, Martin Foley points out that the unions that have done best in winning gains from Labor governments – notably the Australian Nursing Federation and the Australian Education Union – are not affiliated to the party: "The distance they have from the ALP factional system and affiliation arrangements … allows them the freedom and opportunity to both deal with and be seen to take on the government over public sector employment."

And what, in Foley's view, do affiliated unions get from the relationship? Noting that the last twenty politicians the Victorian ALP has returned to Canberra are all "labour movement professionals", Foley writes that there is "no shortage of links between unions and the ALP. It is just that they serve the purpose of getting people into parliament and very little else."

It's time to consider other models that might work better for both the unions and for Labor, and preferably a model in which neither takes the other for granted and each stands on its own feet.

There will be plenty of objections to the idea of abolishing collective affiliation of trade union members, but mostly they will be self-serving. One objection will be financial: the loss of affiliation fees paid by the union. This is not a principled objection, and it is one with which the ALP could cope. Labor is experienced at coping with declining membership fees and declining contributions from affiliated unions. Other sources of funds are available.

In Victoria at present, the ALP's funding comes approximately from the following sources: memberships (12%), unions (24%), corporate donations (30%), individuals (24%) and miscellaneous sources including investments (10%). In other states the figures are similar but may also include subsidies provided to political parties under the Electoral Law. The relative contributions made by these sources have changed over time, and the ALP should not underestimate the potential fund-raising capacity of a larger and more enthusiastic membership. Small but more vibrant parties like the Democrats and the Greens manage effectively without significant union or corporate support.

Other models have provided better outcomes for both unions and political parties of the democratic left. The Swedish Social Democratic Party is perhaps the most successful of its kind in the world. Its philosophy is so entrenched in Swedish life that even during its occasional short spells in opposition it is still regarded as the natural party of government.

The Swedish party began in 1889 as a Labour Party with affiliated trade unions. But in 1990 the structural relationship between the Social Democratic Party and the Swedish Confederation of Trade Unions ended by mutual agreement. A century of collective affiliation of trade unions was abolished because "top trade union leaders had increasingly come to regard the collective affiliation of individual union members as indefensible".

In the decade since, both sides have valued their independence yet there has also been close collaboration. The Swedish Confederation of Trade Unions has contributed important policy initiatives on pensions, skills training, and labour market policy, among others. The party and confederation co-operate in research, exchange of personnel and the publication of newspapers. But neither side takes the other for granted and neither speaks from a position of weakness. In a population of 8.9 million the union movement has 1.8 million members and the Social Democratic Party has 160,000 members.

Similarly, in countries such as Norway and Germany, union movements and social democratic parties have worked together closely and effectively despite having no formal affiliation. A similar arrangement could work in Australia. The devil may be in the detail, but the obvious points of collaboration are in exchange of personnel and in much needed research and policy development.

Within the ALP, reasons are always advanced why overseas experience and models should not be taken into account in considering the future of the party. Other countries have a different history and culture. The most significant difference, however, is that the other models have worked better. The Australian model does not seem to work for either the unions or the ALP.

Party Structure

The Coalition rejoices in federalism. As a constitutional device it suits conservatives, with its built-in checks and balances. It's a colonial structure in a post-colonial age. The ALP advocates a Republic as a symbolic change from the colonial idea, yet it too accepts federalism as its guiding organisational principle. It remains a federation of state and territory branches, a monument to parochialism and conservative values.

Insofar as the Labor Party has a national organisation, it comprises the National Conference, which meets only every three years and is elected by the state conferences, and the National Executive, the chief administrative body. Candidates for the House of Representative are chosen under a system run by state branches, according to rules that may differ considerably from state to state.

This creaky and antiquated structure has not changed in any substantial way since 1902. Both the system of indirect election to the National Conference and the 60–40 rule, in which affiliated unions automatically gain 60 per cent of delegates to state conferences, reject the principle of "one vote, one value" for ALP members, even though the party enshrines "one vote, one value" in its platform as a universal principle of democracy.

The policies of the Federal Party are theoretically determined by the National Conference. But given the three years between conferences, policies are subject to interpretation by the Parliamentary Labor Party and the National Executive. The parliamentary party should not, however, act in defiance of the National Conference without some sort of ratification, such as the Hawke government obtained for the sale of Qantas and for its telecommunication policies. These guidelines are somewhat obscure and not always observed. For example, Simon Crean recently floated the idea of a government subsidy for the purchase of shares in private companies.

Whether or not this is a good idea, it is one which should have the imprimatur of the National Conference, as many delegates may see it as an inappropriate expenditure of taxpayers' money.

In recent years whatever charm these arrangements might once have had has been lost. Conference delegates complain of sterile, "managed" conferences where the outcomes of debates are pre-determined by factional deals. There are few genuine debates. "Unity" as a media offering is preferred to any public disagreement or robust debate.

Rank and File

Local branch members are the foot soldiers of the ALP, but they are not treated like foot soldiers in a modern army. They are starved of weapons, imaginative leadership and good communications. Their ranks are thinning. There are few new recruits other than those pressured into service by the factional warlords.

Any organisation seeking to retain or expand its membership must surely begin by asking: "Why would someone want to join? What's attractive about us? What do we offer?" A national political party should offer an opportunity to influence the political process. Members should feel they belong to a community of individuals sharing common political and philosophical values. A political party on the left, devoted to "the betterment of mankind", has powerful obligations to its members. It should give them a genuine say in its deliberations, free, as far as is possible in any political party, from manipulation, organisational inhibitions and managed solutions. The Labor Party is not such a party and its low membership reflects this fact. Even the Liberal Party offers its members better access to state conference policy deliberations and more say in the selection of parliamentary candidates.

The Democrats' party organisation is more participatory than either Labor or Liberal organisations. The members elect the leader and vote in plebiscites on policy issues. They're not subject to allegations of branch-stacking or "rorting" the system, although their old slogan, "Keep the

Bastards Honest", doesn't appear to have worked as people think politicians are less honest than ever. The Democrats promise "change politics" but have no way of implementing major changes unless they can influence one of the major parties. Nonetheless, they have a larger membership proportionate to their vote than does Labor.

If ALP strategies exist to increase branch membership, they have not been implemented. Attendance at monthly branch meetings is usually poor. In Victoria the *Branch Members Handbook* makes the extraordinary admission that "it is most difficult to attract members to attend branch meetings and the task is even harder to attract them back. Few find enjoyment in the formal procedures of branch meetings." But while the handbook sets out procedural rules for the conduct of meetings, it contains no suggestions for making branch meetings more interesting or for turning them into a "shopfront" that engages the local community. The handbook, like the party rules and the procedures for joining the party, scarcely make party membership an attractive proposition. Until the ALP rouses itself to investigate and apply some options for enlivening branch meetings, meetings will remain encased in an aspic of formality and long-established procedures.

Why, if branches are not catalysts for local community activities, do so many of them meet every month? Could they not meet less often and have better planned and more interesting meetings? Haven't city branches got much to learn from the best country branches, which are often less formal, more friendly and more involved with their local communities? Why do many branches only invite ALP members as speakers? Why not ask speakers representing outside and different interests? Why not ask people critical of the ALP? Why not, I suggested facetiously to one branch, ask Tony Abbott? All the branch members would turn up, the media would turn up, and at the end of the meeting everyone would understand precisely why they were members of the ALP.

The objective is to get people to join and, when they do, to enjoy themselves. In an age of "non-joining", the goal of "mass membership" is perhaps unattainable for a political party. But the ALP can do better at attracting members, especially members who are committed and enthusiastic. As things stand, not much is done by way of membership campaigns. The Wilderness Society, whom one can see recruiting around shopping strips on Saturday mornings, does it better.

The Lesson of *Another Annus Horribilis*: 1977

One night in 1978 I found myself in the dining room of a Mobil service station in Mount Isa. My dinner companion was John Ducker, then vice-president of the ACTU and president of the New South Wales ALP. Ducker was a thoughtful man, a fact he sometimes displayed with an air of bemusement. He and I were in Mount Isa as members of a national committee of inquiry into the parlous state of the Labor Party, and what we were hearing wasn't giving us much joy. At the office of the Australian Workers Union, which represented the workers at Mt Isa Mines, union officials told us that in the federal election the previous year about 60 per cent of the miners voted for the National Party. Nor, in other meetings, had we much joy from other unions or branch members.

That night Ducker and I were both in pensive moods, tired and hungry, as we chose the most attractive item on the menu: a pie, chips and garnish. For a few minutes Ducker seemed lost in thought. Then he pushed his plate to one side, leaned forward across the laminex-topped table and said in his rich Yorkshire accent: "Bruvver, I've got one problem with you."

"What's that?" I asked, a little alarmed.

"I understand", he said, "that you are on friendly terms with a certain Pete Steedman."

Steedman, who later went into federal politics as a member of the Victorian Left, was a noisy libertarian in a leather jacket; Ducker was a conservative New South Wales Catholic. "He makes outrageous attacks on the New South Wales Right," Ducker went on.

I made some comment about the ALP being a broad church. Ducker put on his bemused look and returned to his pie and chips. We were to spend a fair bit of time together as members of that national inquiry, but Steedman was not mentioned again.

After the Whitlam government was tossed out in 1975, the dismissal of the government by the Governor-General, Sir John Kerr, became something of an excuse: Labor had been unfairly treated. But there was no excuse in for 1977 election result. Labor was again decisively beaten. It won just 39.6 per cent of the primary vote, the lowest two-party preferred vote in the House of Representatives in the second half of the twentieth century – the lowest until 2001.

In 1978 the new leader, Bill Hayden, persuaded the ALP National Executive to establish a National Committee of Inquiry into the state of the party. The inquiry was asked to investigate the country's changing social, economic and demographic structure, and how these changes affected Labor's aspirations for a better Australia. It was also asked to look at the most effective functioning of the party, "in terms of maximising the involvement and satisfaction of party members and of communicating the policies and ideals of the party to the Australian community".

The Committee of Inquiry, which I chaired, was a broadly based group. Apart from Hayden and Hawke it included four members of parliament, three academics (who were not party members), three male union officials, a representative of Young Labor and two women, one a union official and the other a teacher.

Together with different points of view and different factional positions, there was also a sense of an important job to be done and a common purpose that transcended ideological differences. The committee received 320 written submissions from individuals, local branches and trade unions. Some members of the committee travelled extensively in order to understand the views of branches and unions in distant parts of the country. There were plenty of discussions with interest groups outside the ambit of the ALP.

The committee published eleven discussion papers covering a variety of topics, ranging from the composition of the National Conference to women's issues, the role of the local branch, unions and the ALP, and social change in Australia.

In 1979 the Australasian Political Studies Association published the papers as a book. Its foreword observed that:

> It has been rare in Australian political history for a major political party to carry out a frank and detailed examination of its own structure, organisation, policies and programs. It has been even more unlikely that a party allows the results of such self-examination to be made available to the public.

In a joint introduction to the book, Bob Hawke and Bill Hayden said that the papers "should provoke consideration of issues which might otherwise be swept under the carpet". And, "the discussion papers raise issues which are continually valid if the Labor Party is to be relevant to Australian society."

In essence the committee recommended abandoning "the Federal Principle" in party organisation. To that end it proposed the direct representation of rank and file members and unions at the National Conference, special measures to develop the representation and role of the ALP in rural areas and in outlying states, affirmative action for women and the revitalisation of the relationship with affiliated unions. It was all about getting light and air into the party.

In 1979 the committee's recommendations were discussed in party forums. Plenty of hostile fiefdoms were threatened by some of the proposals: new party structures, direct representation of members, even affirmative action didn't appeal to people in secure positions who thought things were pretty good as they were. A special National Conference to consider the report rejected the idea of direct representation of members and unions. Instead, as a compromise, it was decided to increase the size of the conference, which gave the superficial impression that it was more representative.

Other cosmetic changes occurred, but in 1979 the enlargement of the conference and affirmative action for women were the main changes to come out of the committee's work. The rest "was swept under the carpet" and the ALP hardly became more "relevant to Australian society".

In 1980 the ALP gained considerable ground in the federal election. Preparing for it distracted attention from party reform. The election of the Hawke government in 1983 led to the comforting assumption that the ALP's organisation must be in good shape. Being in government masks the need for party modernisation.

Yet the discussion papers and report of the inquiry had one good effect. They enlivened the climate of ideas. And some of the less threatening ones were eventually adopted. Under Hayden's leadership, regions were given special attention by the parliamentary party, and strategies were developed for regional Australia. I was given the job of looking after Ballarat and Bendigo in Victoria and the electorates on the coast of North Queensland, the latter with John Kerin, the Shadow Minister for Agriculture. Kerin and I spent a lot of time up there. We listened, talked to local community groups, and published and distributed discussion papers on local issues. In 1980 the ALP won the seat of Ballarat; in 1983 it won Bendigo and the seats based on Cairns and Townsville. In both years there had also been a general swing to the ALP, but a lot of groundwork had been done in these seats.

In the thirteen years of Hawke and Keating governments nobody gave much thought to the party structure, and so the problems remained in limbo. The period immediately after the election defeat in 1996 might have been an appropriate time to review the effectiveness of the organisation. Another opportunity arose after the 1998 election, but the close result convinced the easily persuaded that it was not a time for adventurism. As late as 2000, before the National Conference that year, parliamentary colleagues urged Kim Beazley to take action over the state of the party and put his authority behind the selection of capable candidates in marginal seats. Beazley was a former defence minister: in that role his pulse quickened at the sound of drums, but he was a non-combatant in internal party matters that required a long-term view. He left these matters to factional "leaders" who had neither the authority nor the inclination to do anything.

Many of the recommendations of the 1978 committee, and the discussion papers, remain valid today. Society has moved on but the ALP, as an organisation, has not. In 2001 Bob Hawke and Neville Wran, two of Labor's most successful leaders, have been handed the poison chalice – perhaps more deadly than it has ever been. Their terms of reference are not much different from the terms of reference of the 1978 Committee of Inquiry. They have a big task before them.

Yet reviews undertaken with an ear for community opinion can be very effective. In New Zealand, 52 per cent of Labor Party members are women. At recent elections 9 per cent more women voted Labor than men. Although this result has a lot to do with the Prime Minister, Helen Clark, something more significant is also involved. Much of the New Zealand Labor Party's success in broadening its support base – particularly among women – is attributed to a 1992 party review, "Labour Listens". It was not an internal inquiry but one that involved a range of community groups outside the party. With this review the New Zealand party opened up. In essence it said, "We've got it wrong. We want your views on what you expect from us as a party of reform." It worked because people like to be considered, to be trusted and involved.

What does Labor stand for? As a member of the ALP for the whole of my adult life, I've heard the question asked so many times. It always reminds me of former senator John Wheeldon, a Whitlam government minister and notorious wit, responding to a complaint at a branch meeting that people didn't know what the Labor Party stood for anymore. Wheeldon replied that they were very lucky: "If people knew what the Labor Party really stood for, we'd have no members of parliament at all."

Wheeldon was a cynic at the best of times. He said this after the Whitlam government had been thrown out and (as it seemed at the time) most of Labor's ideas with it. The ALP was trying to work out what it stood for. But Labor's relationship to the history of political ideas has always been uncertain. The reasons are both universal and particular.

Political philosophers are victims of crime. Their ideas are stolen, borrowed, perverted, sometimes trashed or grossly disfigured (Karl Marx and the best of neo-classical economists have much in common, seen from this perspective). Political parties take what bits of ideas they can use in order to get elected and discard what is uncomfortable or just too hard. This has always been true, all over the world, but in Australia political ideas have had a particularly tough time.

Australia was once a pioneer in implementing democracy. Along with New Zealand it was the first country to introduce universal suffrage and the secret ballot. It also initiated the aged pension. Not all its political ideas were progressive – "White Australia" was a peculiarly Australian innovation too – but the first fifty years of this nation's history were built on the belief that national ideas can shape national politics. Early prime ministers like Alfred Deakin and Labor's Andrew Fisher were good at shaping national politics, and they proposed ideas and created institutions that lasted for the best part of the twentieth century.

In the last half-century that pioneering impulse has disappeared. Most ideas in Australian politics now seem to come either from the past or are borrowings from overseas. One important exception is the period between 1966 and 1975 when, after Labor's miserable election defeat, Gough Whitlam set about regenerating the party and ending twenty-three years of conservative rule.

Two lessons of those years remain vital for Labor today. First, Labor is most electable when it has a strong agenda for change. Second, Labor needs to find particular local solutions to particular local problems, solutions that encompass Australia's geographical situation, the nature and diversity of its population and its complex three-tiered structure of government.

The Whitlam story has been well documented, not least by Whitlam himself. But the shortcomings of his short-lived government often overshadow his key role from 1967 onwards in transforming and modernising both the Labor Party and Australian society.

Whitlam's contribution to the slender volume of Australian Political Ideas is threefold. First, he was well ahead of his time in identifying emerging issues. Second, he found new ways to involve outside experts in developing and administering government programs.

Finally, and perhaps most importantly, he wasn't in thrall to overseas models. It was perhaps Whitlam's most famous understatement that "the way of the reformer is hard in Australia." Undeterred, he worked to overcome the constraints imposed by the constitution by developing distinctively Australian ways of implementing programs and policies. He advocated arrangements with the states to give the Commonwealth Government power to introduce uniform standards in areas such as hospitals, housing and railways. He developed the idea of commissions, independent statutory authorities, to advise the government on key policy matters. During his period of government, bodies such as the Schools Commission, the Hospitals and Health Services Commission and the Heritage Commission raised the level of policy debate and the implementation of policy to new heights.

Under his leadership Labor laid the foundations of an independent foreign policy, loosening some of the apron strings that had tied Australia to

Britain and the United States. In 1971 he made his historic visit to China, a visit that was in itself the assertion of an independent outlook. And he argued a strong case for modernising the institutions of representative democracy in Australia, including support for fixed-term elections and parliamentary reform.

Whitlam recognised that Australia was one of the most urbanised societies on earth, that most of its population lived in the suburbs of the big cities. He gave priority to universal health care, to an increased role for local government and to education policies that targeted disadvantaged schools and provided greater access to post-school education. He was the first politician to put urban transport, the liveability of cities and the environment on the agenda of federal politics. The policies he developed were a public sector response to the needs of what these days are called "aspirational voters".

Whitlam succeeded in 1972 for a variety of reasons but chiefly because he seemed the most relevant figure in Australian public life. Having set the agenda, he was seen as the man to implement it.

When the Whitlam government was defeated in 1975, it left, along with a shattered Labor Party, a legacy that highlighted the importance of ideas in progressive politics. Some of the ideas were brilliant, some were ordinary, and a number were not successfully put into practice. But in a unique way they enlivened the political scene.

It is often said, particularly among True Believers, that whereas the Whitlam government was reforming, even visionary, the Hawke and Keating governments were pragmatic and lacking in vision. This is unfair. It is true that the survivors of the election defeats of 1975 and 1977, a number of whom became ministers in the Hawke government, did not look kindly on the policy legacy of the Whitlam government. The shock of the Dismissal, and the indelible memory of high interest rates, inflation and unemployment in 1975, concentrated minds on the issue of economic management. It was the start of a new era in Australian politics, a retreat from the politics of imagination in favour of balancing the books.

Between Whitlam and Hawke, Bill Hayden had the difficult job of repositioning the ALP as a party able to manage both economic responsibility and social progress. There had to be a retreat from both the promise and the excesses of the Whitlam years. New ideas had to be explored within the parameters of a less than robust economy.

Labor's victory in 1983 was above all a testament to Bob Hawke's extraordinary popularity as a contributor to public life. Unlike Whitlam he had no prior history of constructing a broad political agenda; his contribution to ALP policy-making had not been large. But he did have an agenda, revealed and expanded in the early years of his prime ministership, much of which followed from his own background and experience.

Before entering politics Hawke had travelled widely, taken part in international conferences and organisations as ACTU president, and served as a member of various independent reviews of economic and industry policy. He had a reputation as a good negotiator.

Hawke's agenda, and that of most of his cabinet, was to internationalise and modernise the Australian economy. This involved difficult and painful decisions for many traditional Labor supporters. Hawke and his treasurer, Paul Keating, were a powerful combination in generating change. Of Keating, Labor historian David Day has written that "his economic policies … transformed radically the Australian economy and financial system, making it more able to meet the international challenges of the 1990s." This remark can stand as an epitaph for the economic achievements of the Hawke and Keating governments. In a sense theirs was a global vision but it made space for a local agenda that included a wages policy designed to maintain living standards, the preservation of Medicare, the provision of higher and targeted welfare payments and, later, compulsory superannuation and a program for better cities.

Hawke was also an activist in foreign policy. More pro-American than his predecessors, he nonetheless developed with considerable success Australia's relationship with various Asian countries. In the corridors of power in Asian capitals, Australia for the first time came to be regarded as both a friendly and exciting place.

Much of Paul Keating's agenda for economic change had been achieved by the time he became prime minister. This gave him the opportunity to focus on some of the symbolic and emotionally charged issues of Australian nationhood and identity: the Republic, the persistent symbols of a colonial heritage and the dark stain of the treatment of Aboriginal Australians. Like Whitlam and Hawke, he vigorously pursued engagement with the Asia-Pacific region as the place with which Australia's future was inextricably bound.

Few writers about politics have defined Australian social democracy. A vision emerges in dribs and drabs. In articles, in journals and occasionally in speeches, ideas are advanced that seem to hint at a conceptual framework. Cobbled together they can be found in the national platform of the ALP, in the midst of other nice ideas which don't have much to do with political theory.

In the 1990s social democracy became even harder to define. Social democrats had traditionally been concerned (with various degrees of success) with the creation of wealth and its more equal distribution – both within nation states and among the world's population. Fundamental, too, was the maintenance of democratic institutions and values. Ideologically, social democracy had loitered like a foolhardy pedestrian in the middle of the road between the excesses of capitalism and the inefficiencies and totalitarianism of Soviet communism. Then several things happened which demanded a re-think.

In the early 1980s faith in Keynesian economics was gradually replaced by a new economic orthodoxy which had its origins in Britain and the United States. In Britain Margaret Thatcher became "The Iron Lady" of the new orthodoxy. In the United States the new dispensation was called "Reaganomics" and in New Zealand "Rogernomics", after the Treasurer, Roger Douglas.

These ideas had a profound influence in Australia. Roger Douglas became a star guest at conferences of economists and right-wing think-tanks. "Thatcherism" influenced the direction of the Liberal Party. The climate of ideas influenced the economic policies of the Hawke and Keating governments. In Australia the new economics was called "economic rationalism".

Australians, including the author, have sometimes been confused by the term "economic rationalism". When interpreted in subjective and distorted ways, it too has been the victim of crime. Populist critics are better at attacking its perceived excesses than explaining alternatives. If the public policy alternative countenances a country that spends more than it earns, and a government that perpetually relies on budget deficits and fails to acknowledge that economic discipline underpins everything it does, then the critics of economic rationalism are promoting a fool's paradise.

But economic rationalism is usually extended to embrace the idea of the market economy: the market is seen as sufficient in itself. Insofar as a market economy means free trade and competition, it facilitates economic growth, which is mostly a good thing. But free markets are corrupted by governments and corporations. There are social, environmental and human problems for which markets provide no answers. Markets can't respond to starvation, climate warming and terrorism. Markets lead to inequalities of wealth. Even in the narrow realm of economics there is market failure.

The market is like a computer. It has no conceptual capacity, no wisdom, no soul, no morality. The worst enemies of the idea of free markets are those economists who seem to believe that the market can provide universal solutions. Theirs is a form of religion. They believe in the "invisible hand" of the marketplace. The invisible hand leads these gospel economists down strange paths. They become highly susceptible to passing fashions, particularly to theories that seek to justify huge accumulations of private wealth or rationalise abhorrent economic behaviour. "The

Trickle-Down Effect", "The J Curve", "The Twin Deficits Theory" and the idea that current trade deficits are important have been strutted on the catwalk and then disappeared into the used-clothing receptacles conveniently provided by charities for the poor.

Like most vacuous but charismatic religions, this gospel view of the market has followers in high places. Governments have adopted policies on the basis of fashionable theories which have turned out to be flawed. Governments have also become less accountable because their failures can be blamed on the market.

On the coat-tails of hot gospel economists, the community has been bombarded with the idea that the private sector always works better than the public sector, that the role of the public sector is to sweep up the bits, that if there is strong economic growth there's nothing much else to bother about. Such ideas are propagated by economic and financial technocrats who have immense enthusiasm for economic growth and not much else. This is not surprising, because they are among its most favoured beneficiaries.

Such market fundamentalism is antipathetic to the idea of society (or civil society, as it is sometimes called), where citizens act collectively in the common good on the basis of mutual obligations, responsibility and trust. In John Kenneth Galbraith's words, market fundamentalism has led to growing "private affluence and public squalor". It has led to greater inequality and less control of the anti-social actions of individuals. It has corrupted the idea of the public good and replaced collective aspirations for a fair society with narrow individual aspirations. This has been the powerful legacy of Thatcherism, the rejection of the idea of society and the state as representing the common good. Brian Barry describes the Thatcherist legacy in this way:

> It is possible to create a society in which the response to market failure is not a swing to socialism, but an exacerbation of individual efforts to stay ahead by making and spending yet more money.

> Does the public health service have long waiting lists and inadequate facilities? Buy private insurance. Has public transport broken down? Buy a car for each member of the family above driving age. Has the countryside been built over or the footpaths eradicated? Buy some elaborate exercise machinery and work out at home. Is air pollution intolerable? Buy an air-filtering unit and stay indoors. Is what comes out of the tap foul to the taste and chock-full of carcinogens? Buy bottled water. And so on.

The new economic doctrine, and its social consequences, has challenged traditional views of the role of the state. It has challenged the idea of collective action expressed through political ideas and policies, as distinct from individual action, as a means of producing a just society. It has made social democratic parties round the world put their thinking caps on.

As if this was not enough, in 1989 Soviet communism collapsed leaving capitalism, which extols the virtue of competition, with no competition. The global consequences of this emerged quickly, for example with the rapid decline in the level of United States aid to underdeveloped countries.

The triumph of capitalism and huge advances in communications technology impacted on the world at about the same time. The principal beneficiary was the US, the largest repository of both capital and technology. American corporations, many of them richer than most underdeveloped countries, grew in power and influence. The central authority in this new economic order resided with the so-called Washington consensus: the International Monetary Fund, the World Bank and the US Treasury. Insofar as there was authority, it was about as effective as the Keystone Cops. Notions of equity, and of the value of democratic freedoms and sustainable environments, were not embedded in the thought processes of the managers of the Washington consensus in the early 1990s.

The ugly face of globalisation took time to emerge from the shadows. When it did, some leaders of the world's poorest countries thought it bore a striking resemblance to the old colonial system their fathers had told them about. In more developed, small countries such as Australia, the political cognoscenti slowly began to realise the potential limits on the sovereignty and powers of elected governments. A whole range of new pressures would apply to those who did not readily comply with the rules set in Washington about investment, taxation, privatisation and trade.

The social democracies of Scandinavia and other European countries such as Germany and Holland had less difficulty in coping with the new world economy than did the Anglo-Saxon labour parties in Britain, New Zealand and Australia. The European social democracies had long believed in the market economy. They had large companies operating worldwide; they accepted that old industries had to be transformed and believed that with a strong welfare system such changes didn't have to involve massive pain.

Australian Labor's closest relative, apart from the New Zealand Labour Party, is probably the British Labour Party. Does British Labour's response to global change hold lessons for the ALP? Yes and no.

When Tony Blair became leader in 1994, he re-badged his party as "New Labour" and quickly moved to cast off the state socialism baggage of Old Labour. He was young and articulate, a great media performer and wordsmith, with an enthusiasm and self-belief that can sometimes set one's teeth on edge.

Blair's predecessor, John Smith, had taken some steps to reduce union influence at the British Labour Party Conference. In 1995 Blair had the famous Clause 4 redrafted, the Labour Party's historic objective. The old version provided for the "common ownership of the means of production, distribution and exchange". The new version's "aims and values" begins with the statement that "The Labour Party is a democratic Socialist Party," and goes on to refer to "a community in which power, wealth and opportunity are in the hands of the many not the few". The rest of the "aims and values" consists of a series of well-intentioned rhetorical flourishes that seek to define the elements of a civil society.

Blair's biographer, John Rentoul, has described Blair's "socialism" as "ethical socialism, which does not require a belief in rival systems of economic organisation called capitalism and socialism to define it". Lack of such defining beliefs may have been an electoral asset. In 1997 the Blair Government was elected with a huge majority on a program of reform with no clear philosophical underpinning. The philosophy was to come, in government, with Blair's espousal of "The Third Way".

The Third Way is something of an enigma. The name suggests a degree of oriental mysticism, a pathway to enlightenment attainable only by intellectual discipline. Anthony Giddens, Director of the London School of Economics, provided the raison d'être of the Third Way in his 1999 BBC Reith Lectures entitled "Runaway World". In November last year he defended his views in a British Fabian Society booklet, "Where Now for New Labour?" Here he identified several challenges for New Labour including better defining its plans for the revival of public institutions and for building environmental thinking into its core policies.

For some time exaggerated claims were made about the global influence of the Third Way as a political philosophy. Lionel Jospin, the French Prime Minister and Socialist leader, didn't find it appealing. In the United States Clinton toyed with it and dropped it as fast as he dropped his pants. In Scandinavia there was bemusement at Blair's definition of the new way as "modern social democracy" – what had the Scandinavian social democracies been up to all these years?

In Britain, too, it had its critics. The Third Way, wrote Roy Hattersley, a former deputy leader of the Labour Party, "is a lingerie store: customers mix and match to meet their personal taste". It attempts to have the best of all possible worlds, thus enabling the Blair government to accommodate everyone in "the big tent" of British politics.

More importantly, an early version of the Third Way seemed to neglect the idea of equality as a yardstick of social inclusiveness. This was a departure from the past. As the late Anthony Crosland wrote in *The Future of Socialism*, "Equality of opportunity and social mobility are not enough …

they need to be combined with measures to equalise the distribution of resources and privileges."

Tony Blair once said that he didn't mind how wealthy the rich became so long as the poor were getting wealthier too (in Blair's Britain both have become wealthier, though, naturally, the poor less so than the rich). This is a peculiarly British view, coming from someone so used to social hierarchy, so accepting of class distinctions, that the idea of making the poor happier while the rich do as they like fits neatly into an ingrained mindset.

It would be nice to think that in Australia, with its more egalitarian history and traditions, this view would be unacceptable; that it would be better understood that vast discrepancies of wealth demean society and produce more social tension than harmony. But in Australia, too, there is dramatic evidence of a growing gap between rich and poor households. Equality of opportunity is also declining, particularly in education.

The apparent failure of socialism taught us at least one thing. Peter Kellner put it well in a 1999 essay: "Equality of outcome – the same income for everyone – is an impossible and (most would now argue) undesirable dream."

But Kellner goes on to say: "Equality of opportunity is more attractive, but is at best a partial concept, which tends to concentrate on education and training." As Crosland had pointed out years before, equality of opportunity is not enough. Thinking beyond the partial concept of equal opportunity while resisting the feel-good chimera of equality of outcome might be a good topic for enlivening ALP branch meetings. Perhaps ideas will flow upwards.

In the climate of the 1990s politicians of all kinds, but notably for this discussion the politicians of the ALP, have shied away from this hard truth. It cannot be ignored. Equality is not just about incomes. It is about fairer distribution of all those services fundamental to human security and development.

In Britain, debate about equality is now occurring, largely initiated by Blair in a speech to the party conference in late 1999. Blair's new terminology is "equality of worth". It's not as silly as it sounds. For example, its practical application could mean that every citizen enjoys access to good schools and good healthcare, that there are equal political and civil rights for all and equality of incomes between men and women. The emphasis is on rights rather than opportunity. The role of government is, for example, to ensure the right of every citizen to the same quality of education rather than the opportunity for gifted students to attend the best schools.

Some of the gloss has gone off the Third Way. It has not become a new force in British or international politics – one commentator claimed that it was a force only in the minds of Anthony Giddens and Tony Blair. In Europe and the US the right is resurgent, the social democrats again on the backfoot.

Yet it is easy to undervalue the attempts of Third Way thinkers to effect, as Giddens puts it, the "renewal of social democracy". All societies are struggling to cope with the reality of globalisation. Most thinking social democrats accept that any solution must involve a combination of state and market forces. In that process of renewal, the Third Way has helped to create a climate of ideas.

There is not much evidence that the Third Way project has had any influence on the Australian Labor Party at a national level (although some have argued that the Hawke and Keating government policies anticipated Third Way thinking). Publicly, between 1998 and the election of 2001, there were two notable exceptions to this indifference, one on the right, one on the left: Mark Latham, member for Gough Whitlam's old seat of Werriwa, and Lindsay Tanner, shadow minister for communications and member for Melbourne.

Latham embraced the Third Way in a series of papers and speeches between 1998 and today. They contain some interesting, if by no means universally accepted, policy suggestions concerning education, employment and economic management. Lindsay Tanner has been less enthusiastic. The closest he came to Third Wayishness was to write in his book *Open Australia*: "We do not have to choose between Old Left and New Right. There is another path." But, like Latham, Tanner is alert to the changes to Australian society and understands the issues that will be the basis of future politics. "Success in the world", he wrote in *Open Australia*, "will require much greater emphasis on education, information technology and creativity. It will demand the true integration of environmental considerations into the process of government."

Latham, in particular, spoke to a constituency wider than perhaps he or anyone in the federal parliament realised. People with a marginal interest in politics would ask "What about this Latham bloke. He seems to have ideas?" The implications of the question needed no explanation. In the elected silence of the Labor Party hierarchy, Latham and Tanner emerged as the two thinkers of the Opposition.

In November 1998 Latham uttered a warning that turned out to be eerily prescient:

> The Federal Labor Party has made no greater mistake than its decision to turn its back on the Third Way project. It has taken the easy road in Opposition. This puts the Party's electoral prospects out of its own hands, with its reliance on the ongoing incompetence of the Howard government. It is possible that this might not be enough to win the next election ... Labor is in danger of becoming Australia's conservative party – very good in knowing what it opposes, yet not knowing the type of reform it might favour. This is the problem with a policy mix based on retro-economics, producer interests and the old welfare state. It is not likely to inspire optimism about the nation's future.

Without his embrace of the Third Way the first sentence (quoted above) could have read: "The Federal Labor Party has made no greater mistake than its decision to turn its back on *ideas for the future*." The danger for the ALP is that it will continue to react to the conservative agenda rather than spelling out an agenda of its own. This is Latham's point.

Ideas are crucial to an ALP agenda. Ideas are about all the ALP has going for it and they are something which the Coalition has never been good at. Some ideas and examples for the ALP will come from overseas, but history has shown that the best political ideas, the ones which have been successful for Labor, are those developed here in response to Australia's particular circumstances. These particular circumstances include our position in the Asia-Pacific region, a highly urbanised population, multiculturalism, unique environmental challenges and our history including the story of Aboriginal Australia. Within the Labor Party, ideas will only come from a larger and more diverse membership which feels relevant, which feels that it has something to contribute. That's why rejuvenating the party organisation is important.

The party organisation is important for another reason. The ALP has to be able to form alliances with outside organisations with their own progressive agendas. The Adelaide Festival of Ideas in 2001 saw many people, mainly young, representing organisations and advancing individual viewpoints that imaginatively addressed particular Australian problems ranging from water conservation to wealth creation and distribution. A common complaint was that it was difficult to get new ideas into the political process, that ideas were frustrated by political bureaucracies.

Unpersuaded by unreceptive major political parties, these people have nowhere to go politically, no hope of having their ideas put into practice. The same goes for the progressive interest groups that work together under the umbrella description of the "Australian Collaboration", which comprises non-government organisations ranging from the Consumers Association to the Australian Council of Social Services. The Labor Party should aim to form alliances with many of these groups just as it might with unions standing independently from the party. They are all a source for ideas which need implementing.

The ALP's aim should be a new Australian agenda built round the values of social democracy, reflected in policies appropriate to a contemporary society. There is not much point in harking back to Labor's socialist objective, which remains like the Queen and the flag with a union jack in the corner – a reminder of times past. In an easygoing Australian way, the criteria are all there in Chifley's "light on the hill" speech: "better standards of living", "greater happiness for the mass of the people", "working for the betterment of mankind". Chifley was talking about all Australians, not just the relative few who believe that security and happiness can be sold and bought.

Last year saw the publication of two books marking the centenary of Federation. Each book, for different reasons, has a touch of triumphalism about it. *True Believers: The Story of the Federal Parliamentary Labor Party* is a history of the ALP since its entry into federal politics in 1901. It celebrates the ALP's longevity.

The Liberal contribution, *Liberalism and the Australian Federation*, celebrates incumbency in government. Although the Australian Liberal Party is unable to claim a history as long as the ALP's – the Liberal Party having been formed by R.G. Menzies in 1944 – the editors attempt to link the Australian Liberal Party to a longer history of Liberal ideas and values dating back to nineteenth century philosophers such as John Stuart Mill. They claim that in the twentieth century, "the Liberal Party and its 'forerunners' have been in office, in toto, for two-thirds of the period."

The Liberals have always had a terrible hang-up about the attention historians and biographers have lavished on the rich and colourful story of the ALP. How is it, they wonder, that after all those years in office in the twentieth century they have had so little written about them? The problem, apart from their aroma of dullness, is that they only have one icon, Menzies; and Menzies, a cultivated and skilful politician of much gravitas, was at times so pragmatic that it is difficult to distil any coherent philosophy from his many years as a successful politician.

The Liberals' raison d'être has been to oppose the ALP. They have been good at it, and at defending the status quo. At times they have indulged in short bouts of innovation. Menzies' role in establishing the Universities Commission and expanding the Commonwealth role in tertiary education is a good example; so is Howard's in pushing through the GST. Yet the Coalition has rarely espoused ideas that grab the popular imagination. It put forward no new ideas before last year's election.

John Howard's political philosophy goes beyond preserving the status quo: he's keen to turn the clock back. Perhaps the worst decision of the

Howard government has been to abandon the development of better relations with Asian countries. It was a decision motivated by Howard's determination to create a new "old world", in which greater emphasis would return to Australia's relationship with Britain and the United States.

Howard is a clever politician. He's workmanlike, across his subject, articulate. But as he's grown as a clever politician he's diminished in other ways. Is this the fault of John Howard or of the political process? The "Honest John" of earlier years portrayed himself as a local George Washington. He'd never tell a lie or stoop to conquer. Even in 1995 he explained that "truth is absolute, truth is supreme, truth is never disposable in national political life." But subsequent events have revealed him to be no George Washington.

Howard styles himself as a "conviction" politician, but what are his convictions? His favourite list of achievements includes gun control laws, support for the liberation of East Timor and border protection. These were reactions, sometimes good ones, to events that in themselves were beyond his control. They say nothing about convictions or ideas.

Some Liberals found aspects of Howard's election victory last November somewhat distasteful. There can be too much expediency, too much opportunism. Things, they say, will be better when Peter becomes leader.

Peter Costello's natural inclination is to smirk. This suggests a degree of self-satisfaction and the absence of an inquiring mind. As the late Jim McLelland observed, "He who goes through life with a smirk on his face hasn't been looking." People don't like the smirk, the pollsters told the spin doctors, and so Costello's smirk has disappeared; it is suppressed, bottled up, seemingly undigestible. It gives him a threatening demeanour, which could well upset foreign dignitaries at state banquets.

Costello has made the right career moves. Once a barrister, he reads his Treasury brief carefully. His jokes are well rehearsed. He supports a Republic of some sort and reconciliation of some sort. But on the issues of fairness, equal opportunity, Australia's role in the Asia Pacific, some vision for a future society, he's like a fly caught in a web spun by John Howard.

In describing Costello, his biographer Shaun Carney said, there is "only one certainty: his self-belief". So much for "conviction" politicians among Labor's opponents. Their signposts point backwards, down the hill.

What about Labor's rivals on the progressive side of politics, the Democrats and the Greens? In the foreseeable future it is unlikely that the ALP will be able to form a national government without their support. Their preferences in House of Representative elections can determine the outcome. In the Senate they decide the fate of government legislation. Their ideas and organisational principles are important, and the country might be less civilised if they did not exist.

At times ALP members of parliament, senators in particular, wish the Democrats would go away, but they show no sign of obliging. They attract a certain kind of voter, people who see themselves as "progressive" and, by implication, the ALP as locked into old ideas. They have an attractive leader and they produce attractive pamphlets (more attractive than Labor's). They have twenty-three simply stated party objectives that aim at fairness, improving democracy and even at improving the quality of human relationships and animal welfare.

The Greens belong by conviction to a family of like-minded parties and organisations around the world. Their slogan, "Think Global, Act Local", is a clever one. They are attractive to young voters who see them as principled, a party that talks about things people are worried about. And on issues that concern them most they're uncompromising and often right.

In conventional political terms the Greens are categorised as "a one issue party". It may, of course, be the most important issue in the world. But the Greens, impassioned as they are, have not been able to develop a viable alternative political paradigm to the one they legitimately criticise. Even on strictly environmental issues the Greens have been guilty of ad hockery. As one commentator, Professor Boris Frankel, has observed: "Moving to an economically and politically feasible 'Green Economy' is the vague and worthy objective that has never been given a convincing set of programmatic guidelines by Green groups."

Who among these parties is going to be able to build a better Australia? The Democrats and the Greens can't do it. The Coalition won't do it. The ALP remains the sole genuine avenue for political change.

What, then, as Lenin once asked, is to be done?

Last year I attended a meeting of the Fabian Society in a downstairs room at the Victorian Trades Hall. David Feeney, secretary of the Victorian branch of the ALP, was the guest speaker. Feeney is intelligent and has a genial, almost avuncular manner. It's difficult to imagine him as a hard-nosed factional operator, but he is. He talked about the difficulties of the ALP, then he took questions. I preceded my question with a preamble that referred to someone as his factional mentor, an error of fact that irritated him and that he corrected. Later, in answer to someone else's question, he referred in a mildly disparaging though genial way to the views of people he called "the superannuated glitterati".

This was a good put down. As I drove home from the meeting I chuckled to myself and admired its artfulness. And Feeney was right. Too many retired politicians sound off about contemporary politics at every opportunity. They can sound like generals fighting the last war, with little understanding of the dilemmas facing their successors. Each generation of politicians has the task and responsibility to develop policy responses to changing circumstances, with an eye to an imagined future. In policy terms, what's past is past.

If the superannuated glitterati have a role it is, perhaps, to emphasise the importance of continuity. Labor can't be too misty-eyed about its past. But nor should the past be forgotten. It contains important lessons.

In the mid-1990s Gordon Brown, the Chancellor of the Exchequer in Tony Blair's government, co-edited an anthology, *Values, Visions and Voices*, that traces the radical tradition from the time of Oliver Cromwell to the present day. Brown is a man of considerable intellect and firm principles. He's a Scot; he produces good budgets but he also understands the importance of maintaining the radical impulse. His book is an impressive collection of the thoughts and writings of men and women who struggled to transform society and establish the principles and practice of British democracy. Brown appears to see himself as an inheritor of that tradition.

In his last budget in April 2002, Brown began a re-assertion of public sector policy, announcing huge expenditure aimed at renewing the National Health Service. It is to be funded in part by increased taxes. It was a courageous decision and a reminder that social democrats have to take on hard issues.

Brown's book contains a 300-year-old ditty called "Stealing the Common":

The law locks up the man or woman
Who steals a goose from off the common;
But leaves the greater villain loose
Who steals the common from the goose.

Our version is a song about a bloke with a jumbuck in his tucker bag who jumps into a billabong when the squatter and three troopers draw near. How do Australian social democrats continue to reflect the values that Brown espouses in Britain and that inhere in our own different political tradition? How do we carry on the struggle to improve the lives and circumstances of what Chifley called the Mass of the People and to make Australia a fairer place for all its citizens?

Simon Crean has sensibly called for a wide-ranging review of ALP policies. Two difficult issues should take priority. One is the so-called "aspirational voter". The other is the argument that the role of government is finished. These issues are connected. The neo-conservatives argue that everyone would like to be rich and secure. Then they say that governments should move out of the way and let people get on with it, accumulating individual wealth.

The term "aspirational voters" makes some traditional Labor supporters uneasy. "These aren't Labor people," the True Believers say. Rather, these are people desperate to get ahead. Big houses (often with big mortgages), driving the kids to private schools in a four-wheel drive complete with bull-bar, both parents working long hours to make it all happen, regimented leisure, perhaps a beach house with another mortgage, a wad of credit cards, mobile phones for the children … these are the things that make for sweet dreams, and for nightmares.

The nightmares reflect deep insecurity. In the absence of a sense of community, in a society marked by "private wealth and public squalor", the culture of individual contentment may turn out to be an illusion. There is little point accumulating more and more wealth and enjoying it less.

Yet what if aspirational voters are not much different from anyone else? Everyone wants to ensure a good start in life – a good education – for their kids. Everyone wants good health and good hospitals, and everyone wants the things money can't buy: a good physical environment, well-designed cities with safe streets, efficient transport at reasonable cost, reliable public information services and pleasant places to go that reflect the inheritance of the past and the possibility of the future. Everyone yearns for a sense of community, to live in a society in which the things that unite people are genuinely greater than the things that divide them.

In the late '60s and early '70s – before he lost touch with them in government – Gough Whitlam understood the aspirational voters. He saw that people wanted their suburbs and towns to be better places to live in, and he saw a role for public policy in making that happen.

Thirty-five years later, Mark Latham argues that people's primary interests are at neighbourhood level. He advocates "small nuggets of public policy that can improve local schools, clean up the streets and rebuild a sense of community and place". He thinks that government can encourage community values and help civil society where it counts most in people's daily lives. But the policies are yet to come and they need a lot of thought. A government can dole out ideas and perhaps money from Canberra's soup kitchen and it may make some difference, but devolution of power and responsibility is the key issue. It would help if

Labor had a strong local branch structure with members enthused about ideas and pushing them in their communities. That's one reason why organisational change within Labor is important.

An even more pressing intellectual task for Labor is to re-affirm the importance of government. The ALP knows from experience that good economic management – combining low inflation and low interest rates with reasonable growth – is the basis of good government. But government has to be about much more than that.

Galbraith could have been speaking of Australia when he said recently that one of the most questionable distinctions of our time is that between the public and private sectors. "It has concealed the extent to which the private sector, particularly corporate management, has moved to take over or otherwise nullify public responsibility." He went on to predict: "We surely will have an end to freedom from regulation and at least some of the oratory of the magic of free enterprise."

In the past twenty years the balance between the public and private sectors has changed. The public sector has retreated from the management of business enterprises, something it was not always well qualified to do. But the fashionable assumption of the 1990s, that the private sector always does things best and is intrinsically more efficient, is not justified by experience and may now be running up against its limits. The outcomes have been questionable. The economy is more dynamic but the business scene is littered with corporate collapses resulting from a mixture of greed and incompetence. The ALP, as an alternative government, has to work with the private sector but should have no wide-eyed illusions about the capacities of many of Australia's leading businessmen. Corporate misbehaviour inevitably leads to calls for tougher corporate regulation. This can only be put in place by a public sector committed to the public good.

In the last fifteen years, that sense of the public good has been eroded by the damage that governments both Labor and Coalition have done to the quality, corporate memory and morale of the Australian Public Service. The ideal and ethic of public service has been compromised. Last year one of the few ALP policies that crept out from the closet sought to improve the integrity and ability of the public service by restoring some of the independence it had in the past.

A public service committed to the public good is a keeper of a country's corporate memory. The best public servants know what has happened in the past, what has worked and what hasn't. This can be a useful guide to the present and sometimes the future. It is an important part of a healthy democracy.

So too in different ways are an independent judiciary and institutions like the ABC, the universities and a diverse and critical media. Menzies understood this. Latter-day politicians have understood it less. Politicians should respect the integrity of these institutions. The ALP should be a strong advocate of free speech and at every opportunity work to strengthen those values that enlarge democracy.

There is one important signpost which the ALP has always followed and which Coalition politicians have blinked at without understanding. This is the Labor Party's emphasis on determining Australia's own national interest in foreign policy.

From their wholehearted support for Britain in the Suez Canal crisis of 1956, to their support for British and Dutch military action against nationalist movements in former colonies, and for American policy in Vietnam, Afghanistan and now in the so-called War on Terrorism, conservative prime ministers in Australia signed up to the agenda of Britain and then the United States.

The ALP has a different record. From Curtin's World War II stand against Churchill and Roosevelt, to Chifley's understanding of the reasons for revolt against colonialism in Asia, to its critique of the American assumptions underlying the involvement in Vietnam, the ALP retained a sense of Australia's national interest. Whitlam, Hayden, Keating and (to some extent) Hawke reflected this in policies which moved Australia forward and had never been changed or modified until the arrival of the Howard government.

At the dinner in May 2001, when Labor's past leaders were gathered together, Gough Whitlam and Bob Hawke reminded the guests of Labor's record. Whitlam took a swipe at the foreign policy of George Bush. Keating said that, "Emotional cowardice is pushing the Liberals towards America." They "will turn their back on our geography. Their credo is security from Asia, rather than ours, which is security in Asia."

Australia is not respected in the United States. It is taken for granted, and understandably so. In recent years Australia has given a tick to American foreign policy adventurism, however short-sighted and ignorant.

Today Howard is in the toadying business again, identifying Australia's interests with America's. The ALP could feel pressure to follow the same course. If it does so it would be denying its past, when history shows that it has been right and the conservatives wrong in discerning Australia's best interest in its external relations.

Care of the environment also needs a political party committed to good public sector policy. To date no federal government has handled environmental policy well. There's been a lot of ad hockery, but no long-term plan. And, as a result, the Organisation for Economic Co-operation and Development has given Australia a black mark for environmental neglect. Its August 2001 report on the Australian economy points to the economic consequences of neglect and land exploitation: "In the longer run the benefits of maintaining agriculture in its current form … need to be compared with the costs of dealing with resulting salinity and other environmental costs."

The report drew attention to loss of biodiversity and damage to ecosystems, including rivers and the sea. It advocated structural adjustment towards a less greenhouse gas intensive economy, a mixture of special taxes, adjustment of water prices in rural areas, the phasing out of rural and mining fuel tax concessions and incentives for re-vegetation schemes.

These difficult issues are national ones, and, as the OECD report clearly recognises, only a national government will solve them. As Lindsay Tanner has argued in his book *Open Australia*, environmental concerns need to be integrated into the process of government. Tanner called for a national environmental accounting system and a national government prepared to use its muscle to ensure co-operation from the states in dealing with environmental degradation.

These are some signposts that might point the way for a future Labor government. With all due respect to David Feeney, I indulge myself with one specific policy suggestion. The ALP should abandon support for the Pacific Solution as a response to the refugee issue, and the use of detention centres as a punitive instrument of Australia's immigration policy. The first is an overbearing neo-colonial policy imposed on Australia's island neighbours. The administration of the second policy is an Australian disgrace. It punishes the victims of poverty and of tyrannical governments. No votes worth having are to be lost by more humane administration of these centres, by speeding up processes and limiting the time for which people can be detained, perhaps on the British model of day-release schemes. The Immigration Department should be made to pull its finger out.

This is an issue on which the ALP should clearly distinguish its position from the opportunistic policies framed by comfortable WASP-ish lawyers in the present government. It goes to the soul of the ALP and the concerns of the party membership. There has to be a trade-off between capturing the uncertain allegiance of voters, often misled, and retaining the allegiances of a committed membership. At the moment, to regain the fire in its belly, the ALP needs to pay more heed to the convictions of its members.

The problem of refugees is not going to go away. It will only be resolved by international agreement, in which, one hopes, rigorous and more humane standards are set. Labor should commit itself to supporting the best of these standards, not the worst.

All these things are speculative and academic, at least for the time being. Some commentators think they will remain so. Rod Cavalier, a former ALP education minister in NSW, said in a speech not long after last year's election result that the narrow representational base of the ALP put the party on the "route to oblivion". Dr Paul Rodan, a Monash University academic, thinks federal Labor might have too many contradictory and irreconcilable elements for it to win again in its own right. Others have reached the same conclusion.

In politics anything can happen. The ALP could make sensible and far-reaching changes and still not win a federal election. Or it could do nothing and be elected by default. Dr Mackerras's pendulum will no doubt swing again. But a Labor government elected by default will not solve the party's problems or change it into an organisation capable of building a sound agenda for social change.

Some Labor leaders talk of "revitalising the relationship with the affiliated unions" or "conducting new membership campaigns". These things have been suggested before and nothing has happened. Others look back and consider the circumstances in which Labor has won government from opposition in the last fifty years. This has happened only twice, under Gough Whitlam and Bob Hawke. So it might be said the ALP has to wait for the right leader, to wait for its own Godot. But a political party that waits for the unlikely to happen is betraying its membership, its supporters and those who hope for a more democratic and fair society. The ALP can't afford to wait. Waiting lets too many people down.

Others say success will come if Labor tailors its policies to the "missing middle" in suburbia. Again this is possible, but all these things – a new leader, a new sales pitch, the old sales pitch targeted to new groups – will merely provide what Cavalier calls "blue smoke and mirrors" while the ALP remains, in his view, one of "the most undemocratic and unrepresentative parties in the world of parliamentary democracy".

This is too harsh, yet it points to Labor's greatest task ahead. New ideas are important but there is a still more urgent need: the party has to become more democratic. It has to listen again to its members. It must confront the wormwood of the factions. It has to open itself up to new people and new ideas outside the Labor Party, and, as it has done in the past, give political expression to the hopes of progressive groups. Yes, it must honour the True Believers. But it needs new believers, too. They will have to feel included, to believe they are part of a movement for change.

In the 1980s, as a minister in the Hawke government, I used to speak at well-attended meetings at Labor Party branches, including the inner-city one that met in April this year, the meeting that filled me with such despair. I can still picture some of those meetings. The members were often angry, confused by the government's economic rationalism, selling the crown jewels, lowering tariffs. We'd talk about the issues. I'd try to explain. There'd be more questions, and then we'd have the traditional cup of tea and biscuits and talk about other things.

Driving home after these sometimes difficult nights I always felt in a good mood. The Labor government didn't always do as they might have wished, but we could talk things through as members of one party. It was an honour to represent people like these. They had a common belief that Australia could be a better place.

The other day, in a street near where I live, I ran into Lym Fraser. She and her husband Ken have been members of my ALP branch for twenty-four years. They've done the letterboxing, the handing out of cards on polling day, the talking up of the party to outsiders – everything a good party member is expected to do. I asked her if they were still members. She replied, "Yes, I am, but when I rejoined this year I told them on the form what I thought."

She told them that it was not the party she joined twenty-four years ago. It no longer represented people like her. She didn't like the ALP toadying to the electorate when it should have principles of its own that it stood up for. She was talking about federal politics, she told me, because "that's where the real power is."

Did you vote Labor in the last election? I asked. "Of course," she said. "I always do when it comes to the crunch. Some of my friends voted for the Greens but there's no point in that. They can't govern."

Lym and Ken no longer go to branch meetings. "You know," she added, "I think there are a lot of people who think like me, but these days there are more of them outside the Labor Party than in it."

SOURCES

Essay sources and occasional supplementary material are given below. Page numbers indicate where the quotes, etc. appear.

ix C. Hartley Grattan, *Introducing Australia*, New York, The John Day Co., 1942.

8 On Shane Stone, see, for example, 'Costello Demands Answers', the *Age*, 3 May 2001.

8 Tony Walker, 'Three PMs and a Wannabe', *Australian Financial Review*, 9 May 2001.

9 Paul Keating's "forelock tuggers" comment from his speech at the Centenary of the Federal Parliamentary Labor Party Gala Dinner, 8 May 2001. For a full transcript go to http://www.alp.org.au/centenary/pkspcf080501.html.

10 John Howard quoted by Matt Price in 'Federation Celebration', the *Australian*, 9 May 2002, p.6.

10–11 On focus groups and leadership, see Richard Thomas, 'Equality Versus Democracy', *Prospect*, November 1998, p.15.

12 On the lack of difference between the policies of the major parties in the 2001 election, see, for example, '*Australian* Scorecards', the *Weekend Australian* Inquirer, 3–4 November 2001, pp.26–27.

13 Wayne Swan, 'ALP Bid to Neuter Factions', the *Age*, 31 January 2001.

14 Jeff Borland, Bob Gregory and Peter Sheehan, *Work Rich, Work Poor: Inequality and Economic Change in Australia*, Centre for Strategic Economic Studies, 2001, pp.2–3.

15 Quarterly Employment Figures. Statistics on new jobs from the Australian Bureau of Statistics, March 2002.

15 Poll conducted by Irving Saulwick and Associates from 9–15 August 2001. A national sample of 1000 voters, published in the *Age*.

16–17 On political opposition to the government's border protection policy, see Mungo MacCallum, *Girt by Sea: Australia, the Refugees and the Politics of Fear*, Quarterly Essay No. 5, 2002.

18 Gitta Sereny, *The German Trauma*, Penguin, 2000, p.363.

21 On the Health Services Union dispute, see Paul Robinson, 'Unionists Tussle Over $80,000 Payout', the *Age*, 13 April 2002.

24 On youth campaign, see 'The Regeneration of Labor', the *Herald Sun*, 28 July 1999, p.22.

25 On failure of youth campaign, see the *Australian*, 19 March 2002.

25 A fourth seat, Macmillan in Victoria, has a substantial rural component. Of Tasmania's five seats, all held by Labor, one is predominantly rural and two semi-rural.

27 Clarke V. ALP (SA Branch) Hurley & Ors. and Brown.

29 Emily's List comments quoted in the *Age*, 4 June 2002. See also http://www.emilyslist.org.au

29 Susan Ryan's comment on factional allegiances reported in the *Age*, 4 April 2002, p.15.

31 For Bill Hayden's and Barry Jones' comments on the Centre Left, see *Hayden: An Autobiography*, Angus & Robertson, 1996; also quoted in *True Believers: The Story of the Federal Parliamentary Labor Party*, p.262.

31–2 On factional alignments under Hawke, see John Faulkner and Stuart Macintyre, eds., *True Believers: The Story of the Federal Parliamentary Labor Party*, Allen and Unwin, 2001, p.253.

32 Bob McMullan's comments reported in the *Age*, 1 August 1988, and also quoted in *True Believers*.

34 *The Unions and the ALP: 60–40, Factions, Warlordism and Meaningful Engagement*, submission to the ALP Committee of Review from Martin Foley, April 2002.

35 ALP 'National Committee of Inquiry', Report & Recommendations to the National Executive, March 1979.

36 On Australian membership of unions note, however, that membership increased slightly in 2001.

37 For union membership as a percentage of the Australian workforce in August 2001, see Australian Bureau of Statistics findings at http://www.abs.gov.au/ausstats/abs@.nsf/lookupMF/NT000066BE

37 Figure of 57 per cent supplied to the 1978 National Committee of Inquiry by the ACTU.

38 Dean Mighell quote, see Mark Skulley and Stephen Long, 'Head to Head', *Australian Financial Review*, 20 March 2002, p.53.

39 *The Unions and the ALP: 60–40, Factions, Warlordism and Meaningful Engagement*, submission to the ALP Committee of Review from Martin Foley, April 2002.

40 On Sweden: see *World Encyclopaedia of Political Systems and Parties*, George E. Delvin, New York, 1999, p.1063.

46 Australian Labor Party: National Committee of Enquiry Discussion Papers, Australasian Political Studies Association Monograph, No. 23, 1979.

52 David Day quoted in *Australian Prime Ministers*, ed. Michelle Grattan, New Holland, 2000, p.434.

55–6 Brian Barry, *Thatcherism: The Continuing Relevance of Socialism*, Chatto and Windus, 1988; cited in Gordon Brown and Tony Wright, *Values, Visions and Voices: An Anthology of Socialism*, Mainstream Publishing Co. Ltd, Edinburgh, 1995, pp.151–152.

58 John Rentoul, *Tony Blair: Prime Minister*, Little, Brown and Company (UK), 2001.

58 Anthony Giddens's 'Runaway World' Reith Lectures were republished as *Runaway World: How Globalization Is Reshaping Our Lives*, New York, Routledge, 2000.

58 Roy Hattersley quote from 'In the Lingerie Shop', review of *The Third Way and Its Critics* by Anthony Giddens, *Guardian*, 15 April 2000.

58–9 Anthony Crosland, *The Future of Socialism*, London, Cape, 1956.

59 Peter Kellner, 'Bring Back the E-Word', *New Statesman* Essay, 13 December 1994, p.23.

61 Lindsay Tanner quotes from *Open Australia*, Pluto Press, 1999, pp.14–15.

61 Mark Latham, 'Economic Policy and the Third Way', *The Australian Economic Review*, December 1998, p.395.

64 J.R. Nethercote, ed., *Liberalism and the Australian Federation*, Annandale, N.S.W., Federation Press, 2001.

66 Shaun Carney, *Peter Costello: The New Liberal*, Shaun Carney, Allen & Unwin, 2001.

66 Boris Frankel, 'How Useful are Debates on the National State and Globalisation? Australia as a Case Study of the Gaps in Green Theory and Policy Formation', Prepared for the European Consortium for Political Research Annual Joint Sessions, Grenoble, France, 6–11 April 2001. Unpublished draft.

67–8 Gordon Brown and Tony Wright, *Values, Visions and Voices: An Anthology of Socialism*, Mainstream Publishing Co. Ltd, Edinburgh, 1995.

70 J.K. Galbraith quoted by Jonathan Steele, 'The Grand Old Man of American Political Economy Keeps Speaking His Mind', *Guardian*, 9 April 2002.

72 On the OECD Environment Report, see Ross Gittins, 'The OECD Verdict: Our Economy Should Be Greener', the *Age*, 15 August 2001, p.15.

73 Rod Cavalier, speech at Australian National University, November 2001.

73–4 Paul Rodan, Hon. Research Associate in the School of Political and Social Inquiry at Monash University, 'Why the ALP May Be Doomed', the *Age*, 28 March 2002, p.15.

Alison Broinowski

We cannot be reminded too often of our common origins as boat people. We seem to need regular hypodermics of new blood in the national arteries. Otherwise, each generation tends to lapse into smugly preferring sameness and fearfully demonising difference. In his admirable essay, Mungo MacCallum has demonstrated what happens when we have national leaders who are relaxed and comfortable in the afternoon light, idealising the 1950s as a golden age – which for many it was not – instead of challenging us to be interested in change and progress.

Mungo's opening narrative, about the boatload of misguided French and Italians who, unable to found a settlement in the South Pacific, were welcomed by New South Wales Premier Henry Parkes in 1881, is of course intended as a contrast with the Afghans and others refused access to Australia by the present government and its predecessor.

But Mungo misses an important point. In 1888, the centenary year, three ships carrying Chinese – some new migrants, some returning residents – were refused entry to the port of Melbourne and re-routed to Sydney. There, the Chinese were not allowed to land and were expelled by none other than Henry Parkes. Mobs demonstrated outside Parliament House against the ship at the centre of the affair, coincidentally called the *Afghan*. Parkes and the other premiers were already at work on the restrictive legislation that, enacted in 1901, became the White Australia policy.

Rather than holding up Parkes's hospitable gesture to the French and Italians in 1881 as an example of Australia's "compassion and generosity" to asylum seekers, as Mungo does, we should actually compare it with the reverse treatment Australia meted out to Chinese, Japanese, Indians and others. Nothing had changed when Calwell welcomed post-war European migrants while expelling Asian war refugees, some of whom had Australian wives and children. The Menzies government urged Australians to "Bring out a Briton" in the 1950s and

1960s, as Mungo notes, while refusing Asians residency for "economic" reasons. Asian students in the more liberal 1970s and 1980s still had landlords slam doors in their faces, and *all* the dozens of Asian Australian writers I have surveyed have been called names like Ching Chong Chinaman. In the late 1980s, John Howard wanted less Asian migration. In the 1990s, racial insults were still common on Australian streets; and Pauline Hanson echoed her Queensland constituents in calling for signs in Asian languages to be banned. We have passed laws against racial vilification that Howard and his ministers appear to ignore when they say what they claim are Muslim cultural practices make asylum seekers unfit to become Australians. John Stone wants only "Judaeo-Christians" as migrants.

Governments in the 1990s and 2000s still clearly display the same double standards as Henry Parkes. Visa overstayers from Western countries are virtually ignored while "illegal immigrants" from the Middle East are imprisoned in remote detention centres. The Navy was mobilised to pick up lone French and British yachtspeople, but armed SAS troops were sent to board the *Tampa*, loaded with Muslims. Australia seeks to attract Asian students to our schools and universities but many in China, Indonesia and Vietnam are now finding it exceptionally hard to get visas. Australia selects prospective migrants in Asian countries according to employment categories, and then puts them through the qualifications run-around when they arrive. How many white farmers from Zimbabwe have fled to Australia, compared to Indians from Fiji? How many migrants have brought their prejudices with them?

Australia's perennial hypocrisy about immigration doesn't negate Mungo's point that individual leaders don't share it, and that it's not characteristic of the entire community. It's just that our "compassion and generosity" towards new arrivals was never evenly distributed to non-Europeans. He could have cited the *Afghan* episode to show how depressingly little has changed, in spite of appearances. Australian politicians may claim that their policies treat all migrants equally, but they know they treat some more equally than others.

Alison Broinowski

Gerard Henderson

This is a revised and expanded version of an article that first appeared in the *Sydney Morning Herald* and the *Age* on 26 March 2002.

As the maxim goes, on occasions no cause is seemingly lost until a certain individual or organisation publicly joins it. Like, say, the leftist commentator Mungo MacCallum.

Right now, the shelves of Australian bookshops contain two new tomes by Mungo MacCallum. Namely his memoir *Mungo: The Man Who Laughs* (Duffy & Snellgrove, 2001) and *Girt by Sea: Australia, the Refugees and the Politics of Fear* (*Quarterly Essay* No. 5, Black Inc., 2002). In the former, the author declares that he is "one who has remained committed to the ideals of the left". In the latter, he opines that, "if it is by their Acts that you shall know them, [John] Howard deserves the name of racist."

As he makes clear in his memoirs, Mungo MacCallum remains a political activist – albeit with constrained aspirations. Once he believed that the left could change the world; now he contents himself with the hope that "Byron Shire just might be … ready for the left". This might surprise visitors to the enclave in north-east New South Wales where discussions of property prices seem as obsessive as in Sydney, Melbourne or Brisbane.

Two issues emerge from the Ocean-Shores-based activist's attack on the Prime Minister. Is the put-down politically smart? And, is it true? But first, some history.

Speaking in the House of Representatives on 8 October 1996, John Howard claimed that "early in 1992" he had been "bucketed … as racist" by Paul Keating. However, there is no evidence in the *Hansard* that the former Labor prime minister had ever called John Howard a "racist". Nor is there any newspaper report or transcript to support the allegation. Nor has the Prime Minister's Office been able to back the claim with documentary evidence. It is true that, during an interview with John Laws on Sydney Radio 2UE on 21 January 1992, Paul Keating criticised the Coalition's policy on Asian immigration of some years previously (when John Howard was Opposition leader). But he did not mention Howard by name and he did not use the "r" word.

Now, few would dispute that John Howard is a very clever politician. Moreover, like the rest of us, he would not enjoy being termed a racist. So, why did the Prime Minister claim that the insult had been used against him in public by Paul Keating when, in fact, this was not the case? Who knows? But it is possible that the politically astute John Howard may believe that there is some benefit in being labelled a racist by your political opponents. It's all about unintended consequences. The perpetrator of invective may believe that an unflattering label will always do damage. Sometimes, no doubt, this will be the case. On other occasions, the allegation may prove counter-productive. There is evidence that Australians do not like being called racist. If this is the case, then it may be that the use of the "r" word as a term of abuse actually reinforces established beliefs about immigration, multiculturalism, asylum seekers and so on. It is much the same with the debate over Aboriginal reconciliation. References to past genocide, however well intentioned, are invariably a turn-off.

In *Girt by Sea*, Mungo MacCallum makes a number of sensible points about Australia's history as an immigrant nation. Namely that "the Sydney of the 1940s was already a multicultural society" – the same could be said of Melbourne. What's more, there is considerable evidence to support his claim that, "given face-to-face contact, Australians remain tolerant and easy-going about race – if their politicians give them half a chance". And he is correct in comparing John Howard's occasional stridency with that of Bill Hughes – rather than Liberal Party founder Robert Menzies. None of these points is new – all are well made.

Yet, every now and then, *Girt by Sea* goes over the top. For example, there are references to detention centres as "isolated and degrading gulags" and to Alexander Downer's "gulag archipelago". Clearly legitimate criticisms can be made of mandatory detention in Australia – which, as Mungo MacCallum acknowledges, was introduced by Labor – and of the Coalition's so-called "Pacific solution" for asylum seekers.

Yet, whatever may be said about Australian detention centres, they cannot properly be compared with the forced labour camp system invented by Josef Stalin to maintain the Soviet Union's repressive state. The terms "gulags" and "gulag archipelago" were popularised by the Russian writer Alexander Solzhenitsyn to describe the reality of labour camps in the totalitarian communist system. They have no valid application to contemporary Australia. Not if words are to have real meaning. In serious debate, hyperbole is not helpful. It's too easy to dismiss.

There is considerable evidence that the administration of mandatory detention in Australia is in dire need of reform. The policy was administered harshly by former Labor ministers Gerry Hand and Nick Bolkus (both of the left faction, no less) and even more harshly by Immigration Minister Philip Ruddock. But mandatory detention in Australia, however reprehensible, should not be equated with the worst excesses of Stalinism.

When discussing the issue of "whether Howard himself is a racist or not", Mungo MacCallum reverts to a cliché: "If it waddles like a duck and it quacks like a duck then it probably is a duck; it's certainly safest to treat it as a canard." The evidence for so serious an assertion is based on John Howard's August 1988 comments – where he called for a reduction in the Asian component of the immigration intake. And on his statement during the 2001 Federal election campaign – namely that "we will decide who comes into this country and the circumstances in which they come here."

Well, on these criteria, the label racist could also be thrown at quite a few of Australia's Labor leaders. *Girt by Sea* makes no mention of Ben Chifley. Yet, as David Day points out in his biography *Chifley* (HarperCollins, 2001), in November 1928 the ALP hero lamented that "Australia was supposed to be a white man's country but Mr Bruce and his Government were fast making it hybrid." Ben Chifley's chief complaint about Stanley Melbourne Bruce and his colleagues was that (allegedly) they had given "preference to Dagoes – not heroes". At the time, Chifley wanted to defend White Australia from even southern Europeans, including Italians and Greeks. The tactic appears to have worked. The Coalition lost seats to Labor in the November 1928 Federal election.

Later, as prime minister in the late 1940s, Chifley supported Immigration Minister Arthur Calwell's decision to deport refugees from Asia who had settled in Australia. Some had served with Australian forces during World War II. As David Day comments, in the late 1940s, "the Labor Party seized upon a handful of Asian refugees who had been allowed refuge in Australia during the war and who had married Australians and who were now resisting repatriation." The *Wartime Refugees Removal Act* was introduced by the Chifley government to facilitate this end.

Girt by Sea is critical of former Labor leader Arthur Calwell. But not of his successor, Gough Whitlam. MacCallum records that in 1975 Whitlam "famously declared" that he was "not having hundreds of fucking Vietnamese Balts coming to this country". The source (which is not provided in *Quarterly Essay* No. 5) is Clyde Cameron's *China, Communism and Coca-Cola* (Hill of Content, 1980). The quote has not been denied.

Cameron also recorded that Whitlam had rejected the plea of Foreign Minister Don Willesee that "Vietnamese who had been employed by the Australian Embassy" should be granted entry as refugees. Willesee was also defeated in his attempt to allow "re-entry to students who had returned to Vietnam after completing their studies in Australia". Clyde Cameron, who was Minister for Labor and Immigration during the first half of 1975, supported the Whitlam position. According to Mungo MacCallum this "was one of the few occasions when the Left, including its charismatic leader Jim Cairns, gave Whitlam unswerving support". That's all he says.

Mungo MacCallum rationalises Gough Whitlam's 1975 position by describing his mention of "Vietnamese Balts" as "a reference to previous escapees from communism who invariably voted for the conservatives". In other words, Whitlam did not like the fact that anti-communist refugees/displaced persons, who had settled in Australia from Eastern Europe after 1945, tended to vote for Robert Menzies and the Coalition. He was determined to deny anti-communist Vietnamese admission to Australia because, according to his view, they would also support the Coalition.

To MacCallum, this is reason enough. But is it? The fact is that it was the anti-communist Vietnamese who were the refugees/asylum seekers in 1975. They were the ones who lived in genuine fear of persecution following the fall of Saigon to Hanoi's Soviet-supplied forces in 1975. The Whitlam government wanted to keep genuine Vietnamese refugees out of Australia in 1975 – because the Prime Minister of the day and some senior Cabinet members did not like their politics. This stance was totally at odds with Australia's international obligations.

Just imagine what Mungo MacCallum would have written in *Girt by Sea* if John Howard had made a similar comment about, say, Muslims. Just imagine that a reliable Cabinet source had revealed that the Prime Minister had declared circa 2001: "I'm not having hundreds of fucking Muslims coming to this country with their religious and political hatreds against us." Just imagine. In his memoirs MacCallum refers to warnings he once received from Richard Walsh that he was heavily into idolatry of Gough the Great. On the available evidence, the condition still exists.

It's much the same with Bob Hawke. In November 1977, just before the Federal election of that year, the HMAS *Ardent* intercepted a boat containing some 180 Vietnamese refugees, heading for Darwin. Bob Hawke was ALP Federal president at the time. In words that sound remarkably similar to John Howard's over two decades later, the (then) ALP president opposed the arrival on Australian shores of queue-jumping boat people. Bob Hawke told a media conference in Hobart on 28 November 1977:

> Obviously there are people all around the world who have a strong case for entry into this country and successive governments have said we have an obligation, but we also have an obligation to people who are already here ... Of course we should have compassion, but people who are coming in this way are not the only people in the world who have rights to our compassion. Any sovereign country has the right to determine how it will exercise its compassion and how it will increase its population.

Bob Hawke was reported as calling on the Coalition government to make it clear that the asylum seekers had no right to land in Australia. Fortunately Prime Minister Malcolm Fraser rejected his advice. He said that Australia needed to make sure that the Vietnamese boat people were refugees but felt that the situation was under control. You can read all about it in the broadsheet press of 29 November 1977 and after. But, alas, not in *Girt by Sea*.

It is true that Bob Hawke was not alone in calling for a tough line on asylum seekers a quarter of a century ago. According to a contemporaneous report in the *National Times* (12 December 1977), Hawke's position was shared by senior Fraser government minister Peter Nixon. The Coalition Transport Minister was reported to have told a media conference that refugees arriving illegally by boat in Australia would be turned around and sent back. Peter Nixon was quickly hauled into line and the Immigration Minister (Michael Mackellar) issued a statement declaring that, "Australia will continue to accept Indo-Chinese refugees." The Fraser Government went to the December 1977 Federal election with this policy.

The (then) Labor leader's position was ambiguous, to say the least. Gough Whitlam never repudiated Bob Hawke's statement. Moreover, while acknowledging that "any genuine refugees should be accepted", he maintained that "the Government has a responsibility to ensure they are genuine refugees" and that "it should also see that they don't get ahead in the queue over people who have been sponsored and who are already coming here" (*Age*, 29 November 1977). Sounds familiar, eh? The *National Times* reported that, speaking in Darwin, Whitlam had blamed Lee Kuan Yew for the boat people reaching Australia's shores. He was quoted as alleging that Singapore supplied the Indo-Chinese boat people with the "plans and petrol and the maps to get here" (*National Times*, 12 December 1977). Shades of November 2001 when some Coalition political operatives hinted that Indonesia was directing boat people to Australia.

Soon after joining John Howard's personal staff in January 1984, I spent time in the Parliamentary Library digging up the evidence concerning the stances taken by Bob Hawke and Gough Whitlam when the boat people arrived in Australia after the end of the Vietnam War. I gave this material to John Howard and he used some of it in his speech in the House of Representatives on 23 August 1984. On that occasion Howard took a strong stance for immigration and opposed any attempts to use boat people/asylum seekers to win political points during election campaigns – as Labor had done in 1977.

Subsequently John Howard changed his position on immigration and, eventually, asylum seekers. In separate radio interviews on 1 August 1988 with John Laws (Radio 2UE) and Paul Murphy (ABC Radio PM), Howard maintained that "the pace" of Asian immigration "has probably been a little too great" and advocated that Asian immigration to Australia should be "slowed down a little" in the interests of what he called "social cohesion". In a written statement, issued on 11 August 1988, John Howard specifically quoted Bob Hawke's 1977 comments in support of his position, viz.: "Any sovereign country has the right to determine how it will exercise its compassion and how it will increase its population."

I did not agree with John Howard in August 1988 or November 2001. Or with Bob Hawke in November 1977. Or with Gough Whitlam in mid-1975. But I do not believe that the actions of any one of these men warrant the accusation of "racist". In *Girt by Sea* Mungo MacCallum maintains that, due to his various acts, "Howard deserves the name of racist". But he ignores Hawke's acts of 1977. And he simply refers to Whitlam's acts of 1975 as "famous". Instead there is reference to the fact that Gough Whitlam wrote to Labor leader Kim Beazley on 4 September 2001 rebuking him for failing to carry out Labor's policy concerning Australia's international obligations with respect to asylum seekers/refugees. Whitlam's letter (which was quoted in the *Sydney Morning Herald* on 12 November 2001) also criticised previous governments – including the Hawke and Keating administrations – for not doing enough to bring about the implementation of various human rights conventions in this area. Yet the fact remains that when Gough Whitlam had a chance to be magnanimous about refugees/asylum seekers in the mid-1970s he conspicuously failed to grasp the opportunity.

From time to time various governments, Coalition and Labor alike, have acted without empathy concerning refugees. At other times they have demonstrated considerable compassion – especially the administrations headed by

Malcolm Fraser (November 1975 to March 1983) and Bob Hawke (March 1983 to December 1991). Mungo MacCallum, correctly, acknowledges the successes in this area of the Fraser and Hawke years. And MacCallum is quite realistic about the fact that Kim Beazley and his advisers had little option in 2001 but to support the Howard government's pre-election legislation. He maintains that the belief that the alternative would have amounted to "electoral suicide" is "probably right".

Girt by Sea also makes the valid point that John Howard used the issue of asylum seekers – following the *Tampa* affair and the genuine concern about terrorism after the events of 11 September – as the core of the Coalition's election campaign. Clearly the Prime Minister and Liberal Party Federal Director Lynton Crosby exhibit some self-doubt about the legitimacy of this tactic. Which explains why, after the event, both have attempted to establish the myth that the election was not fought on border protection. It may be that, after *Tampa* and 11 September, the Coalition could have defeated Labor without running on the asylum seeker issue. Maybe. But that is not what happened – and Mungo MacCallum is correct in drawing attention to this.

It's just that, at times, *Girt by Sea* goes over the top. The term "racist" does not adequately fit any Australian prime minister – past or present. What's more, as John Howard recognises, branding those who exhibit little empathy for asylum seekers as "racist" does not do real harm to the non-empathetic brigade. Such an insult is sometimes readily worn as a badge of honour. Similarly demonstrations outside detention centres, which sometimes turn violent, do not help the asylum seekers' cause. Symbolic politics may be enjoyable for those involved but rarely produces constructive outcomes.

As the German sociologist Max Weber understood, successful democratic politics is about slow boring through hard boards. In so far as the case against Pauline Hanson's One Nation has succeeded, this was brought about by moderate argument supported by empirical evidence. Not by (verbal) fire of the this-I-believe genre in *Green Left Weekly* or even the *Byron Shire Echo*.

As the modern Labor Party understands, the left's critique has little to offer those who want to bring about social change in democratic societies. Even in the Byron Shire.

Gerard Henderson

John Hirst

The *Tampa* episode was very revealing of the state of Australian society and politics. Seventy-five per cent of the Australian people supported the Prime Minister in not allowing the *Tampa* people to land on Australian soil. The left-liberal intelligentsia was appalled at the Prime Minister's action, which they saw as mean, heartless and damaging to Australia's international reputation. They were ashamed of their country.

Their denunciations continue to flow. Two issues of *Quarterly Essay* have now been devoted to this issue. Last year Guy Rundle issued *The Opportunist: John Howard and the Triumph of Reaction*. Now Mungo MacCallum has produced *Girt By Sea: Australia, the Refugees and the Politics of Fear*.

The critics offer two explanations of the episode. Firstly it revealed that multiculturalism was a veneer and the Australian people had reverted to type and were as xenophobic and racist as they had been when they supported the White Australia policy.

The second prong of the explanation is to blame it on the man who took the decision that was so widely supported. Howard, it is said, is unfit to be a prime minister; he is a crude populist willing to do anything to save his own skin.

In sum, the *Tampa* episode reveals that a nasty man is in charge of an ugly people. The proponents of this explanation evidently find it highly satisfying. I don't.

As Paul Kelly has pointed out in the *Australian*, Howard's critics refuse to take the question of border protection seriously. Rundle dismisses it in an aside – "5,000 or so arrivals by sea did not present any sort of logistical problem" (p.6). What numbers would present a problem; whether the 5,000 safely arrived would encourage many more to come, Rundle does not consider. The Labor government of Paul Keating thought it had a problem because it decided to put asylum seekers in detention camps, an action not attributed to the character failings of the Prime Minister.

John Howard did not, as his critics allege, "create" the refugee problem when the *Tampa* entered the scene. Handling the refugees was a long-standing problem for the government. In 1999 it set up a special taskforce to deal with the issue. It was administering a law that it thought was inadequate and could not change to the extent that it wished. The number of unauthorised arrivals was rising. Since the *Tampa* refugees had hijacked a seaworthy vessel and directed it away from Indonesia and towards Australia, the Prime Minister could act decisively. This incursion was both more blatant and more readily repelled.

The popularity of his firm stand and the wrong-footing of Labor on the issue gave the Prime Minister a great electoral advantage. His critics claim that he should not have taken it, for it let loose a wave of xenophobia and racism. I have seen no wave. No doubt the action was welcomed by the racists and xenophobes, but for most of the supporters the claim that they were moved by racism or xenophobia is implausible. The attitudes that have made the great migration such a success do not change overnight. The migrants, including a quota of refugees, are still coming. During the election campaign the Prime Minister did not bring the migration program into question; on the contrary he continued explicitly to support it. To characterise as xenophobic a country that is running a large-scale, non-discriminatory immigration program is a contradiction in terms.

The Prime Minister's slogan for the campaign was: "We will decide who comes into this country and the circumstances in which they come here." Note that it was not: "We will have no migrants." Nor was it: "We will send the migrants home." These would have been the cries of a genuine populist. His words were: We determine *who comes here*. This minimum claim for the sovereignty of the nation is denounced as xenophobia and racism.

For its supporters, the Prime Minister's action was a highly reassuring event. Its broad appeal was not to race or xenophobia; it was a declaration that Australia still existed and could still take charge of its destiny. (Whether in fact it will be able to control the flow of boat people remains to be seen.)

There are strong forces leading us to feel that Australia is slipping from us. There is the imperative to compete in a global economy and to adapt ourselves to "world's best practice" which involves the abandonment of long-established Australian policies, a course to which both major parties are committed.

There is also the sort of multiculturalism that insists that Australia should not be defined. Australia is a mixture, a process, a becoming. Among the Liberals, Rundle prefers Jeff Kennett who he claims genuinely saw community as "a work-in-progress undertaken by different ethnic groups – a community of no particular or specified character" (p. 25). One of Rundle's gravest charges against Howard is that he is confident about what Australia is.

Australia is also erased by those who claim that it must unquestioningly follow all UN declarations and treat unauthorised arrivals as if they were already citizens. About the rights of these people the civil libertarians are amazingly tender. The ordinary citizen is mostly locked out of the courts, but an illegal arrival, declared not to be a refugee, must be able to carry their case to the highest court in the land.

The issue of the boats arriving on the north-west coast is essentially one of control. The Prime Minister demonstrated that someone is in charge; that Australia has a view on its migrant intake; that it has interests and processes that it wishes to protect. The critics who say that the numbers are few forget that Australia is already running a large immigration program, including the reception of refugees. That program has its perils. For the multicultural zealots a migration program can do no damage; it is a self-evident good; once begun it can never be scrutinised, reassessed or stopped. But the great majority of Australians want the government to keep an eye on what is happening. The relationship between support for the Prime Minister on *Tampa* and the general immigration program is the reverse of what Howard's critics imagine. A tough stand on border control *increases* support for the official migration program.

Mungo MacCallum is the latest critic not to understand this. He knows Australia well; he notices that even in the 1940s and 1950s Australians had an easy tolerance for newcomers. His mistake is to think that those attitudes must have disappeared in Australia in 2002 because most Australians supported the Prime Minister on *Tampa*. Like many others, he thinks Indonesian fishing boats organised by people-smugglers are the modern equivalent of the boats that Arthur Calwell arranged for the Displaced Persons. Why Australians should accept the one and reject the other is a genuine puzzle for him.

There is no evidence of change in Australian attitudes to migrants who are already here or those invited to come. The critics of Howard were ashamed of their country. It is now time for them to be ashamed of themselves – for so misunderstanding and denigrating their fellow citizens.

John Hirst

Postscript: On 7 May 2002 the Howard government announced that the migration intake for next year would rise to 105,000 (from 93,000) and would be maintained above 100,000 for the next four years.

Philip Ruddock

Australia's treatment of asylum seekers and refugees has come under close scrutiny over the past two years – since the introduction of Temporary Protection Visas in 1999. There is generally great passion but, unfortunately, limited balance in the public debate on these matters. Critical issues are too often viewed narrowly and out of context, with little appreciation of the global context within which today's humanitarian crises occur. Mungo MacCallum clearly has much passion, but that passion appears to be limited to the people who have the opportunity and resources to confront him. We can search his essay for references to and concern for the people living in appalling conditions in the camps in drought-ravaged Africa, having fled fighting in Sudan and Sierra Leone. Perhaps we could expect concern to be voiced for the women who are raped and beaten as they compete for firewood and fodder for their animals. We can seek references to people digging open latrines in over-crowded camps in the Middle East and West Asia. It is a vain search. The people I refer to will never have the money that will make them interesting to people smugglers. They will never confront us and, unless we seek them out, we will never hear their story.

There is a certain naivety and distortion in MacCallum's approach. Rather than pick every item or deal with individual cases, we can examine and quickly dismiss a few points where the facts are beyond doubt and then put this issue into its proper context.

MacCallum mocks warnings that 10,000 people could be on their way to Australia (p. 37), yet well over 10,000 people have arrived or attempted to arrive since late 1999 and it is fairly clear that some thousands were still ready to arrive before the Government took firmer action.

MacCallum starts delving into myths and holding up people who arrive by boat as heroes when discussing the terminology used (p. 42). MacCallum will be disappointed to learn that the term "boat people" is still used, but it is misleading to suggest that every boat arrival is an asylum seeker or that every asylum seeker is a refugee. Look at the situation in Europe, where about half a million people claim asylum but only about 10 per cent of them are found to be refugees. We can put that alongside the claims that all asylum seekers are detained (the majority are free in the community), or that someone who arrives without a visa is not breaching our law and hence, the term in the Act, an "unlawful non-citizen". I do have a concern, however, that by applying the term "refugee" to all unlawful arrivals, commentators devalue the term and diminish the trauma and loss of sanctuary that refugees experience.

The "hero" approach is further extended by the attitude taken towards the people rescued by the *MV Tampa*. In one line (on p. 49) we see the dismissal of the actions of people who put a captain and crew under duress. They had been rescued and were en route to an Indonesian port where they would have been safe, but it appears to be of little moment that they effectively forced the ship to turn around.

Trying to imply Australia's approach to the *Tampa* and wider issues is somehow racist ignores the simple fact that over the past five years Australia has welcomed migrants from more than 180 different nations. It also ignores the reality that Australia's refugee and humanitarian program is still resettling people from the Middle East, West Asia and Africa. These are not the actions of a xenophobic, racist community.

The Global Context of Australia's Humanitarian Policies

A democratically elected government's overarching responsibility is to the nation it represents – and this includes making decisions about international engagement. In this regard, the basic decision is how to engage the international community. Or, in other words, defining the breadth of international engagement. For example, governments decide what conventions, treaties and agreements are signed, what aid and assistance is provided, what bilateral relations are developed and how the nation participates in multilateral forums. These choices reflect the moral, ethical and compassionate stance of the nation.

Australia was one of the first countries to sign the 1951 Convention on the Status of Refugees and remains committed to the implementation of the Convention and its 1967 Protocol. Australia has provided refuge and support to more than 600,000 refugee and humanitarian settlers since the end of the Second World War and continues to provide the opportunity for 12,000 people to come to Australia under our Refugee and Humanitarian Program each year.

Our focus in recent years has been on Africa, the Middle East, West Asia and the Balkans. Australia's multicultural society has ensured that refugees from all parts of the world can settle in Australia with safety and dignity. Australia continues to work with the UNHCR and other countries to ensure that the international protection system delivers durable solutions in a timely, efficient and fair manner to those refugees who need them.

Australia's Contributions to the International Humanitarian Effort

The reality of budgets, other resource constraints and competing priorities means that a subsequent set of decisions governments make relates to the depth of commitment – overall and within each element of its international engagement strategy. These decisions will take into account the entire spectrum of national responsibilities – humanitarian, social, economic and environmental.

Constraints and competing priorities are a fact of life. There are limits to the resources governments have at their disposal and hard choices have to be made.

While there has been some focus recently on the funding for Australia's approach to unlawful arrivals, we need to put this in context. It is estimated the United Kingdom spends around £2 billion (more than $A5 billion) each year on processing and catering for asylum seekers. It was recently reported that its litigation budget was around £129 million (more than $A300 million).

Developed nations around the world spend at least $US10 billion each year handling half a million asylum seekers, of which about 10 per cent will be found to be refugees.

All this at a time when the UNHCR is struggling to reach its core budget target of $US800 million, and remember it is dealing with more than 21 million refugees and people of concern. This imbalance is quite simply obscene.

It is also difficult to get governments to focus on the possibility of becoming refugee resettlement nations when their resources are already stretched in dealing with thousands of people making asylum claims on their border.

There will always be some disagreement between various parties as to where limits should be set but there is no doubt that the capacity of Australia, or indeed of any country, is not unlimited. Australia can't help all 21.7 million refugees and people of concern throughout the world, but we do demonstrate every year that we will continue our efforts to assist those most in need.

In a democratic society a representative government sets the limits, taking into consideration a range of views, including from other levels of government, lobby groups and academics – even philosophers. No matter how passionate (or compassionate) a government, group or individual may be about a particular issue, responsible policies should always take into account the practical limits of what can be done and the impact on other policy areas and, more broadly, on the nation.

To ignore the critical role of government policy in humanitarian matters is to ignore the reality of finite resources and their distribution. Even unlimited compassion has limited impact unless it can manifest itself in good works. Good works require resources and the efficient and effective allocation of resources is at the core of good government policy. There is no compassion in failing to manage asylum and refugee policies properly and losing community support. There is even less compassion in reducing your ability to help those in the most vulnerable position.

Every element of our international strategy should be managed according to the resource limits within which it is set – including the provision of resettlement places as a durable solution for refugees. No one could reasonably expect any country's offer of resettlement places to be open-ended.

There are similar considerations regarding aid, assistance and financial contributions to international organisations. In this, we cannot responsibly make open-ended offers – but we do set generous limits.

Australia is among the thirteen largest donors of financial resources to the UNHCR's core budget. In addition, we have contributed to special appeals from time to time to assist with particular crises, including the recent crisis in South-West Asia. In the past two years Australia allocated some $53.8 million to assist with the situation of Afghan refugees and displaced persons. These commitments have supported the delivery of essential food, education and protection services to Afghans, as well as supporting the UNHCR in its co-ordination role in responding to the crisis. The Government will continue to monitor the situation of the Afghans and other refugee populations to ensure that it provides support where it can. It has already set aside a further $12.8 million over the next three years to address the humanitarian needs of displaced Afghans and Iraqis, both in countries of origin and in countries of asylum in the Middle East and South-West Asia.

Targeting Australia's International Humanitarian Programs

Having decided the scope of how Australia will participate in the international humanitarian effort and having allocated generous resources, the Government must make a third set of decisions before implementing its policies and programs. Who will be the recipients?

The Government's asylum, protection and resettlement policies are purposefully designed to focus on the most vulnerable. Those who seek asylum get access to process and those who need protection are given effective temporary protection while the appropriate durable solution is sought.

Asylum seekers who enter Australian territory are afforded access to asylum processes of the highest standard, including the option to seek review of a primary decision. The fact that these processes may be conducted outside Australia is irrelevant in the context of international obligations. It is a truism that asylum seekers are people seeking asylum. Their primary objective should be to access appropriate processes – and not to access a particular territory. Seeking access to a particular territory is a migration goal.

Individuals who go through asylum processes and are assessed as being in need of protection are duly afforded that protection pending resolution of a durable solution. This is the core obligation of the 1951 Refugees Convention, embodied in Article 33 – "No Contracting State shall expel or return ('refouler') a refugee in any manner whatsoever to the frontiers of territories where his life or freedom would be threatened on account of his race, religion, nationality, membership of a particular social group or political opinion." The specific location in which protection may be provided is irrelevant. The primary objective of a refugee is finding effective protection. It is not about getting access to a particular territory or to particular benefits.

Then, having provided process and protection, the Government, with the co-operation of the international community, seeks to facilitate the most appropriate durable solution for refugees. It is at this stage that matching refugees' needs to the international community's capacity to respond takes on a special significance. It is at this stage of the process that good government policies are vital. It is at this stage that scarce resources must be targeted with care and compassion.

An overriding question critics must answer is why people who have the resources and the opportunity to confront us should have a greater call on our compassion than those languishing in appalling conditions in refugee camps and who have no money to buy a people smuggler's services. We must also listen to those whose voices cannot be heard in Australia.

UNHCR considers that repatriation (return to the person's country of national origin, in safety and dignity) is the preferred durable solution – and the Australian Government fully supports this view. Where repatriation is not possible UNHCR considers that local integration (settlement in the country of first asylum) is the next best durable solution – and the Government agrees.

However, for a relatively small number of refugees neither repatriation nor local integration is appropriate and UNHCR seeks resettlement (permanent residence in a third country) for refugees in these circumstances.

The intended recipients of resettlement places in Australia's programs are chosen from those for whom there is no alternative. Australia's offshore

Humanitarian Program targets refugees in camps who cannot go home and who cannot be integrated in their country of first asylum – refugees with no resources to hire a people smuggler and who can offer no protest but silence.

Globally, resettlement places are limited – only about 110,000 per year are available in a handful of resettlement countries. The international community must use these places responsibly. Governments and UNHCR must decide who gets a resettlement place. This cannot be a self-selection exercise undertaken by asylum seekers nor can it be left to people smugglers to decide.

Only by retaining control of the system of international protection, including determining which refugees are in need of resettlement, can the international community ensure that the finite collective resources of governments are allocated effectively and efficiently. This is the only realistic and constructive approach – and one that reflects rational compassion.

Over recent years the Humanitarian Program has been set at 12,000 new places. Places used in the program are used for asylum seekers in Australia found to require protection under the Refugees Convention as well as refugees resettled from offshore. In the past year under Australia's Humanitarian Program, 13,733 people were given visas for Australia.

Alternative Approaches

The alternatives do not stand up to scrutiny. Some commentators seem to imply that engaging a people smuggler and undertaking a dangerous sea voyage is evidence enough of an individual's desperation and, therefore, of their refugee status and a need for, and a right to, permanent resettlement. They seem to suggest that all unlawful arrivals in Australia are refugees and should be resettled here permanently.

How would a government implement such a policy? Would we simply take the first XX thousand each year that managed to get to the border and turn away the rest? Or would we simply take all who decided to come and preside over the dismantling of an orderly refugee and migration system that has served the national interest and maintain our international obligations? As part of such a policy, would we ignore as "collateral damage" the refugees in camps who need resettlement but cannot pay a people smuggler – those who can offer no protest but silence?

How could a refugee resettlement policy based on principles like "first come, first served" and "survival of the fittest" ever be construed as being compassionate or equitable for the most unequal and the most vulnerable?

Many have advocated approaches taken in Europe and North America where people are released into the community, but we can learn significant lessons from their experience. The UK recorded some 88,000 asylum applications in the past year. In an interview with *Lateline* on 15 May, British Shadow Home Affairs Minister, Dominic Grieve, when asked to comment on the British system of allowing people into the community, said:

> Well, I'm afraid it doesn't work. The evidence of that is overwhelming ... last year 88,000 applicants, 10 per cent granted asylum, 25 per cent given leave to remain, but only 9,000 people actually leaving the United Kingdom ... the evidence is overwhelming that there are very large numbers of people coming into this country, claiming asylum, not getting asylum but remaining here.

A report in the London *Telegraph* on 19 May 2002 suggested that more than 270,000 failed asylum seekers had disappeared into the British community.

A Fact Sheet on the US Immigration and Naturalisation Service website reads: "89 per cent of non-detained individuals with final orders of removal failed to surrender for deportation when ordered to do so."

On the 10 January 2002 the French magazine *l'Express* published a report on a French government document that estimated up to 95 per cent of all asylum seekers had disappeared into the community.

With that weight of evidence and more, I find it hard to be convinced that Australia should follow the leads being demonstrated through the alternatives when they undermine the very integrity of the global refugee and humanitarian system.

Conclusion

When considered in the context of the global humanitarian crisis and a world where governments are daily constrained by finite resources and multiple priorities, the Australian Government's asylum and refugee policies are a pragmatic and compassionate approach.

We fully meet our international obligations with respect to asylum and protection by providing access to proper processes for asylum seekers and effective protection for refugees. Furthermore, we endorse the principle that repatriation is the preferred durable solution, we commend and support countries of first asylum and we reserve permanent resettlement in Australia for refugees who have no other option – those who cannot return home or have not found safety in their country of first asylum.

Philip Ruddock

Angela Shanahan

It is hard to know where to put Mungo MacCallum on the spectrum of political commentary in Australia. On the one hand there are sober, unbiased political journalists whose opinions are read and noted in the highest echelons of government: Paul Kelly, Laurie Oakes, Michelle Grattan and, yes, even Alan Ramsey. Down the other end are the various loudmouth, up-yours, know-alls who have managed to push their way onto the airwaves and into the commentary pages of newspapers. I know that is where Crikey dot com puts me. But where does one put Mungo?

Mungo is a professional of long standing, but at the same time he does have the burden of being known as a "character". When I was in my teens, Mungo was known as an oddball who would suddenly appear on television to deliver jeremiads against the (usually) conservative government of the day. He was never dull, and he certainly made an impression in our house. My father, whose Italian background and profession as opera singer means he usually only watches SBS at 2 a.m., suddenly said about a year ago after one of Mungo's now infrequent appearances, "Angela, who *is* the bloke with the beard and the voice?"

To be blunt I am beginning to suspect that Mungo is redundant and that isn't just because of the ancient hippy aura. It would account for the almost incoherently shrill tone of the essay *Girt by Sea* as well as its bizarrely unsubtle and unhistorical overview. Mungo's vision is of an Australia divided into the pre-Howard and post-Howard era. Biblically denouncing "Howard's debauch" as he calls the government's policy on illegal entrants, Mungo conjures a vision of a bumpy but successful multicultural Australia turned into nasty, racist, anti-immigrant Australia almost overnight, lured by the hellish Hanson's siren call. Apparently we have all succumbed to racism freed from the constraints of good manners, as he calls the prim political correctness of people like him. The Australia of his boyhood, where a bit of good-natured banter about "reffos" was to be expected and which under the guiding tuition of the benign elite commissars of PC was evolving into a cosmopolitan Utopia, has been betrayed by racist "aspirationals" or as he sees it just plain greedy voters.

Sounds bad. How could this collective madness have happened? Mungo knows about the experience of what I among others have called the elites alright, but of the immigrant and "aspirational" experience he knows nothing. For in Australia they are one and the same. Mungo's weird before-and-after-Howard scenario is the product of a reasonably affluent childhood in the eastern suburbs of Sydney and of a career of misreading Australia through the narrow prism of the left, closeted in Canberra and unwilling to look beyond its rigidly imposed definitions and boundaries. Australia has changed – but not in the way he thinks it has.

Firstly the Australian immigrant experience of Mungo's boyhood described in the first part of his diatribe is told from his own deliberately sanitised perspective. Redleaf pool is not Lakemba or even the MIA. There were plenty of immigrants in Australia before the '50s and Mungo deliberately glosses over that experience in order to exaggerate what came after.

Whatever one thinks of the treatment of illegals in Woomera, probably the lowest point of the immigrant experience in Australia (bar Lambing Flat) was the detention of "enemy aliens" in World War Two who were bona fide immigrants. Some of them had endured familial separation for many years in the quest to come to Australia. My father was nearly ten before he set eyes on his father who had left Italy when he was six months old (and if you think this is the cynicism of the old wave of immigrants concerning the experience of the new, you'd be right!). When Mungo was splashing about at Redleaf, it was common for immigrants speaking a foreign language in the city's streets to be abused. Mungo didn't think that the term "reffo" was too offensive but we don't hear anything of the opinions of those on the other end – and I write as someone who was periodically called a wog at school in the 1970s.

Mungo employs all the clichés and misconceptions that he can to conjure a very roseate view of post-war Australia, irritatingly citing John O'Grady's cloyingly awful book *They're a Weird Mob*, which contains every stereotyped misconception about Italians that was ever invented. He blithely characterises any dissatisfaction with immigration as just pub talk (page 18). The experiences of some of us who are the products of an earlier generation will testify that it wasn't all pub talk. But so what? We got over it. But Mungo is forced to sanitise much of the immigrant experience so as to make the post-Howard "debauch" look even more luridly, well, debauched!

The fact is that new immigrants generation after generation have struggled to find and hold their little bit of Australia and it is usually a very grudging accommodation on both sides. Frankly, immigrants don't care about the "welcome mat". They want to acquire as much as they can for their families and they want to be left alone to do it. These are unashamedly aspirational values, even though Mungo from the safety of the old establishment thinks it is simply "greed". He, like so many of his caste, is torn between his leftish, cosmopolitan, multicultural, call it what you will attitude to immigrant culture, and his inability to acknowledge the very raison d'être of the immigrant, which is the aspirational mentality (or greed) that he so despises.

He quite rightly points out that Australia absorbed new refugees from Indochina not, I think, because we were imbued with some newfound principles of multiculturalism (Gough Whitlam famously called them Asian Balts), but because they came from a communist country against whom we had fought a bitter and protracted war. They were our allies and we owed them. It was that simple. But Mungo has no evidence to support his claim that Australians generally agreed with Hawke's impulsive announcement that we would take the Chinese students. Most people were shocked at this soapy grandstanding which reduced government policy to prime ministerial fiat. I couldn't see any reason to take the sons and daughters of a lot of Chinese apparatchiks when we had already started to detain and return other boat people.

It's at this stage that Mungo starts to get muddled because his whole thesis depends on the nastiness of the Howard government's detention policy, and of course Labor introduced it. So he comes up with an explanation which involves a form of mass psychoanalysis. We apparently were becoming a terrific cosmopolitan place with cappuccino and falafel on tap but still this nasty undercurrent of racism could not be quelled by the concerted efforts of the enlightened to instill political correctness. The odium of all politically correct thinkers was concentrated on the One Nation party as the representatives of the dark side. Keating, we are told, "would have hammered One Nation into the ground like a tent peg". How? What legislation would he have invoked? But more's to the point, why? Doesn't Mungo trust Australians to make their own decisions on the matter, as the eventual demise of One Nation shows that they have?

Ah, and there we have it. Obviously not, because according to Mungo's interpretion they can't. They voted for Johnny. They didn't listen to the people who knew so much more about politics and society – the people who invented all those handy isms – especially multiculturalism. In short they didn't listen to the "elites". It is difficult to know why the left hate Howard so much. But this in the end is what Mungo's essay boils down to. Perhaps it's the *suburban* symbolism of Howard. For the well-educated, thoroughly indoctrinated, left-leaning products of the '60s, he represents everything they thought they were rebelling against. Ironically, it shows up the extent to which that rebellion was a product of a real cultural cringe – the cultural poverty of a clique of journalists cut off from the suburban heartland. Howard is not cut off. His feeling for middle Australia transcends cultural divides, because he understands the things the aspirational are aspiring to. The old left like Mungo (who ascetically scorn those "things") are reduced to impotent foaming fury in his wake.

If Mungo wants to know what elitism is, he should look in the mirror. No one is using the term intelligentsia as a term of abuse, but I have decried the *phoney* intelligentsia. (Well, when the word is applied to people like Phillip Adams, one doesn't know whether to laugh or cry!) But would not Professor Blainey, one of our most interesting and respected historians, count as intelligentsia? Nonetheless, he was abused for nothing more than expressing an unfashionable opinion.

However, what is really quite scary about the attitude of the old left is their manipulatively maudlin, phoney "compassion" which has nothing to do with real people and everything to do with political symbolism. As Jean-Marie Le Pen said in an interview a few weeks ago, the immigrant has replaced the worker as the symbol of oppression for the left. And frankly the immigrant is giving the left the same raspberry the worker did, as demonstrated by the results of the last election, particularly in western Sydney. But apparently some people cannot see the dehumanising effect of turning people into symbols. This is precisely what Mungo and the anti-Howard journalistic push has done by using the suffering of a little boy to further *their* political ends.

As a resident of Arnclifffe in Sydney's south for ten years, during which time a mosque was built, it was annoying to have people make stupid jokes about our regular suburban neighbourhood becoming little Beirut, particularly since we and our like-mindedly "aspirational" Lebanese neighbours seemed to have pretty much the same "look after your kids, fix up your house and wash your car on Saturday" values. One of them, Jusef, once remarked to me after he noticed I was waddling around with baby number seven, "Angela, you got so many kids you could be Lebanese!" Like everyone else in Sydney, we spent more time thinking about interest rates and house prices than politics. Since then I have moved to the most extraordinary city on earth, Canberra. Meanwhile back in Arncliffe house prices have gone up and much to my neighbour's relief the renters have moved further west – to the new little Beirut, where all sorts of mayhem is rife. However, back in Arncliffe neither Ali or Jusef are, I suspect, too sympathetic to the Woomera detainees.

So where does this leave Mungo? Redundant, that's where.

Angela Shanahan

Robyn Spencer

Reading Mungo MacCallum's *Girt by Sea* makes me realise that I live in a different world from Mungo's, with different life experiences, heroes and villains, a different view of history and different loyalties. But we and our children will share the *same* future.

As a typically left-wing, politically correct journalist who views history with a black armband and sees and chronicles crimes I cannot see, Mungo draws bizarre conclusions about legal and illegal migrants, the *Tampa* episode and John Howard. Any despondency Mungo feels about all the above, and especially about lack of journalistic vigour, is unwarranted. After all, his side is supported by nearly every journalist and media presenter in the land, once again a point of difference in perception.

The post-World War II immigration program occurred when Australia was a very different country from today. We had a small population, even considering the environmental constraints of the world's oldest and driest continent. Our cities were not overpopulated and polluted, Sydney was delightful, we did not have one of the world's highest per capita foreign debts and thus could afford the infrastructure necessary for an Australian standard of living. We needed affordable labour and lots of it in order to develop our manufacturing industries and government infrastructure projects. Mungo says, "the newcomers were not, of course, reffos … the essential point was that they were different, but by and large acceptable."

Of course early Anglo/European immigration was acceptable because these people immigrated under a policy of assimilation and, most importantly, were from the same Western Christian civilisation as our own. Our cultural differences were superficial. We shared beliefs in freedom of speech, democratic rights, democratic elections, law and order and the separation of government from public service, as well as an appreciation of an egalitarian society. Migrants had a willingness to learn about and become part of their new country.

Australian people understand that Australia is now in a very different position from the '60s and early '70s. But big business and humanitarians have run and continue to run the big growth agenda. The effect of population growth on our scant and dying river systems and the fact that we have no permanent snow fields to feed them is ignored. Our pre-glacial history ensured that we have the world's oldest, least fertile and thinnest soils, and the demands made on the land to produce more are put into the too-hard basket. Technology will fix it, is the cry.

No independent study has shown that economic benefits result from mass immigration. But one study concluded that immigration is "benign", a conclusion that resulted from ignoring the major costs of immigration-infrastructure provision. Even Paul Keating in his 1970 Maiden Speech to parliament said, "It is time we considered the enormous cost of bringing migrants to this country." He commented that it would be better to spend money on child endowment than on immigration.

There is no concern that under the policy of multiculturalism, an evil policy of division, our nation is being divided into Blainey's "nation of tribes". Australians are sick and tired of the constant denigration of our culture while the virtues of every other culture in the world are extolled. We are witnessing our precious tolerant Australian culture and our unique way of life becoming just one culture among many. The glue of a common national memory that holds us together as a nation is disappearing as we become a *multicultural land inhabited by global citizens in a geographical place in a borderless world*. Mungo will be happy about this, but the Australian people from many backgrounds are not.

Mungo, you miss the point. The people have been totally divorced from the political process in immigration matters. As Bob Hawke said in May 1993 when he was an ex-prime minister, "There has been an implicit pact between the major parties to implement broad policies on immigration that they know are not generally endorsed by the electorate, and they have done this by keeping the subject off the political agenda." He also said that, "... the implicit pact between the parties in regard to immigration could not have been achieved without the acquiescence of the ACTU leadership". (See Katherine Betts, *The Great Divide: Immigration Politics in Australia*, Duffy & Snellgrove, 1999.)

Bipartisanship equals *no debate*. The people have no say because both major parties agree to agree with each other! Big business, ethnic community leaders, multinationals and bleeding hearts want bipartisanship to continue; the people do not. Australian people live with the daily consequences, including witnessing university places being given to foreign, fee-paying students rather than to our own qualified youth. Australian workers face unemployment due to massive overseas skilled migration and I question the morality of attracting skilled people trained in developing countries to Australia simply because it is cheaper than training our own. The list goes on.

Yet Mungo MacCallum was "shocked by the sheer ferocity of the public reaction against the boat people". Mungo, you really need to get out into the real world. The public's reaction to illegal arrivals has several components. It is not difficult to understand the resentment against queue jumpers (and yes, Mungo, that is just what they are when our government adjusts the official refugee acceptance numbers for those applying offshore *down* according to the numbers accepted onshore) and the reaction to the bullying and blackmailing tactics used by illegals, not to mention the destruction of tax-payer-provided facilities.

Refugees coming to Australia over the past twenty years have been an enormous drain on our welfare system. Australia has accepted this as our contribution to a worldwide problem. However the reality of 2002 is very different. The integrity of our entire program is under threat from illegal economic migrants and the greatest threat to all Western nations is now from the mass movement of people, legal and illegal.

We only have to consider the words of Dr Mahathir when he said in the *Australian* (7/5/97) that "we should migrate North in the millions, legally or illegally" and "masses of Asians and Africans should inundate Europe and America." It's interesting that Dr Mahathir himself has just deported 900 illegals, yet he has allowed, in a hostile act to Australia, his country to act as a conduit for people leaving safe third countries of asylum to aim for Australia. The hostile acts of both Malaysia and Indonesia must be confronted by the Australian government or else the entire "Pacific solution" will be futile.

The difference between Mungo and myself, as representing the conservative nationalist point of view, is that I believe in the nation state. The internationalists' support for globalisation, with their belief in the free movement of capital, goods, services and people, means the ultimate destruction of the nation state with its concepts of borders, sovereignty, identity and even democracy. The only threat to internationalism is nationalism.

We are on opposite sides. There is a new fault line running though Western nations, all of which are being subjected to the same immigration-related phenomena as Australia. This new fault line is not a line between "right" and "left" but between those who stand for their nation and their civilisation on the one hand and those who stand against them and for "New World Order", immigration and multiculturalism.

National conservative or "right-wing" parties are now influencing the governments of Austria, Denmark, Portugal, Belgium, France and Italy. The bloody assassination of Pim Fortuyn in Holland should be creating a time of intense reflection for all Western peoples. The people in most Western nations have been subjected to an internationalist hostile media, browbeaten by their own governments and by the pinko left social point of view. Pim Fortuyn questioned immigration, legal and illegal, and also its devastating effects on his Dutch culture. Why shouldn't he? The frustration of the ordinary people is that only one side is heard and any attempt to explain another point of view is treated with violence and hostility. Do not think it hasn't happened in Australia. Look at the Hawthorn Town Hall meeting for One Nation in 1998. I organised this meeting and the bloody scenes instigated by the "left" to stop the meeting were a national disgrace. In Australia now we cannot even hold a meeting. The rights to free assembly of people and freedom of speech have been removed by the thuggery and violence of the "left" with media and government approval.

But Mungo, have no fear. Reality for you is much kinder than the scenario with which you sadden yourself. Sure, Howard dragged himself back from political oblivion using the refugee issue. He wanted to win an election.

Refugees coming by boat uninvited and demanding entry provoke hostility. If someone in the street *demanded* a dollar from you, you would resist. If someone asks for a dollar with a hard luck story, they have an excellent chance of getting the money. So it is with refugees.

A hostile response to demands and blackmail is natural and so thought 80 per cent of the Australian people. Refugees coming at our invitation do not create such hostility. Howard captured the hostility, was swept into office and simultaneously grabbed most of the One Nation votes back. He cleverly damaged the only electoral threat to the Liberals, the political "right" known as One Nation.

A disenfranchised public is not really concerned whether the children were thrown overboard or not. Mungo again seems surprised that "the public attitude to the asylum seekers hardly changed" while people "marked politicians still lower on trust". The fact that our laws are being flouted by those passing through safe third countries and arriving on our shores attempting to blackmail the host people through their unbelievable behaviour trumps even politicians' lack of credibility.

One Nation questions the stupidity of helping 0.05 per cent of asylum seekers/refugees at huge expense while ignoring 99.95 per cent left behind. Surely it would be preferable for Western nations to increase foreign aid massively to help the majority? A policy of temporary refuge for those under direct persecution with a policy of return, paid by the Australian people when the situation in the homeland is resolved, is a far fairer one.

Howard does not care one hoot if 3,000 extra people, Asian, black or whatever, come into Australia legally or illegally. The entire *Tampa* performance was for public consumption and they fell for it in droves.

If Howard cared about control of our borders, why is there no action on the seventy-three people per day who have come through our airports for the last twenty years and stayed illegally? There are 500,000 illegal overstayers living in Australia today. The government tells us it is only 60,000 but anyone with Grade Three maths can go to the Australian Bureau of Statistics, obtain their figures for annual arrivals and departures to and from Australia, subtract one from the other, make a few simple corrections for refugees, migrants, expatriates and New Zealanders etc. It is all there in the official figures. But both sides of politics and the media do not want to know about this and don't care anyway.

One Nation believes Australia must withdraw from the 1951 Refugee Convention, as this would enable us to develop appropriate responses to current world refugee problems. For Australia to be constrained by a Convention signed half a century ago has become absurd. The 1951 Convention was designed to cope with events such as World War II in Europe. No one in the early 1950s could have predicted the situation in the world today with at least 100 million seeking migration outcomes, a minimum of 4 million attempting to migrate illegally each year, let alone the estimate of at least 23 million genuine refugees worldwide. In today's world we should formulate a refugee law around the right to return rather than a right to remain.

Mungo, your anxiety and depression about the situation should be relieved seeing that the Liberals have just increased our immigration intake massively and in a way that will give every Asian studying in Australia a migration place. So you cannot sustain your view that John Howard is anti-Asian, xenophobic or against high immigration. He is following your vision for Australia, he is presiding over the largest Asian immigration component in our history.

The punters whom you call aspirational voters and who want immigration decreased have just voted Howard into power!

What is more, the Liberals will probably soon elect Peter Costello to replace John Howard. Well, Mungo, be happy again. Costello is your man. He believes in a Republic, "sorry" statements, Asian immigration, high immigration, multiculturalism, the lot! Indeed, I would swear, in all the things you believe in. Paul Keating reincarnated!

The Mungo MacCallums of this world constantly judge the past from the perspective of the present and make judgements on the actions and motives of men in the past, whom they then categorise as morally deficient or evil. If this is acceptable, then it must be acceptable for the past also to judge the present. As most of the speakers from the distant past are now dead white males, let me speak on their behalf. Arthur Calwell is a good example. A man now denigrated, but in his time considered by both his side of politics and his adversaries as a decent, just, patriotic, principled and unpretentious man. By his standards, he was socially and economically "left". But by today's standards, Calwell would be socially "right" while being "far left" economically. Menzies would likewise today be considered socially "right" and economically "left" when compared with current ALP or Liberal Party leadership.

The probable next leader of the Liberal Party, Peter Costello, is the mirror image, or inverse, of Arthur Calwell or Robert Menzies – "left" socially and "far right" economically. What does this make the current Liberal Party leadership compared with decent, just, patriotic, principled and unpretentious leaders of the past? To Calwell and Menzies, Peter Costello would seem an inexplicable aberration from all that they held dear, as would Simon Crean.

Mungo, from the perspective of 2002 you judge our past harshly, but from the perspective of the past, your views would be regarded as simplistic, irrational and destructive. Who is right?

Time will tell.

Robyn Spencer

Mungo MacCallum

First, a confession. Two otherwise complimentary readers have pointed out that I was quite wrong in referring to the incident on the Lambing Flat goldfields as a massacre. In fact although the Chinese miners were twice attacked by mobs armed with picks and shovels and their huts burned, none were actually killed. The aim was to chase them off rather than murder them. I am happy to make the correction and find it interesting that my critics on the right have been so eager to castigate what they see as my errors of opinion that they missed this glaring error of fact.

But perhaps this is typical of those who might be described as the sneering classes; their aim is to win the argument by any means available, not to engage in serious debate. With the exceptions of Alison Broinowski and John Hirst, those complaining about *Girt by Sea* are less interested in what the essay actually said than in the fact that it was written from what they see as a left-elitist viewpoint. The mere thought that I was brought up in the eastern suburbs of Sydney and now live on the north coast of New South Wales is sufficient to discount it.

So perhaps I should make what in parliament would be described as a personal explanation. The eastern suburb in which I spent most of my formative years was Paddington at a time long before it was gentrified. The neighbours were almost all working class – what would now be called battlers, or at best aspirationals – with a generous sprinkling of Greek and Italian migrants. During the years I worked in Sydney I lived first in Ultimo and later in Birchgrove, again before the trendies moved in to either suburb. I ventured forth across the city, yes, even unto the wilds of Angela Shanahan's stamping ground of Arncliffe, and since then have travelled extensively around Australia and beyond.

It has hardly been a sheltered existence. I find it a little difficult to understand why this background, combined with a philosophy of rational scepticism, should be assumed to produce a narrower world view than that of critics such as Mrs

Shanahan, a conservative Roman Catholic who believes Canberra to be the most extraordinary city on earth. But enough self-justification; back to the debate.

I greatly respect Alison Broinowski's knowledge and commitment in the area; we have had spirited discussions in the past. But I still cannot go along with her pessimism; the idea that an unbroken thread of racism runs through Australian immigration policy and any departure from it by politicians or outbreak of tolerance in the community should be treated as an aberration.

It is certainly true that up to and before the end of the White Australia policy the official policy towards non-Europeans was one of unqualified rejection, and that even after the implementation of non-discriminatory criteria there were pockets of prejudice; old habits die hard. But given sufficient encouragement from the top they eventually succumb, and I would maintain that they were well on the way towards doing so before the emergence of One Nation and its tacit acceptance by John Howard. Since then, of course, it has been all downhill.

But the fact remains that Australia is now a de facto multicultural society with an increasing proportion of Asians and non-Christians; the pattern is irreversible. Sir Henry Parkes wouldn't have liked it; Pauline Hanson, John Stone and, I suspect, John Howard (despite his recent protestations) still don't. But I have no doubt the majority of Australians are pragmatic enough to come to terms with it – as long as our leaders give them the chance. We still have some distance to go, but we have come a long way since 1888.

It is always reassuring to find oneself on the other side to Gerard Henderson, a commentator whose employers at The Sydney Institute are too ashamed even to identify themselves. There, that's out of the way. Since Henderson likes to open his critiques with a personal insult it seems only proper to reply in kind.

Henderson focuses his attention on my assertion that John Howard deserves the name of racist, and immediately gives his priorities away by claiming that two issues emerge from the assertion. First, is the put down politically smart, and second, is it true? It may surprise The Sydney Institute, but there are still some of us who believe truth is more important than political cleverness; to whom the question of whether or not the Prime Minister is in fact racist matters more than whether or not we can score a debating point by saying so.

Henderson worked for Howard for a time, and his own insights into what motivated the venomous campaign against the boat people would be useful. Unfortunately, he chooses to dodge the issue and shoot the messenger instead.

Henderson claims my only evidence is Howard's 1988 speech on the need to reduce Asian immigration and his Hansonesque slogan which adorned the polling booths of the nation on 10 November. More assiduous readers will remember I also cited the Wik legislation which deprived Aborigines of rights found to exist by the High Court, Howard's evident discomfort at the 1997 Reconciliation Convention, the praise of One Nation's David Oldfield (and, it now turns out, the French National Front's Jean-Marie Le Pen) and his failure to respond to the charge that he would never have treated white, Christian asylum seekers in the way he treated Iraqi and Afghan Moslems. The case relies on Howard's actions as well as on his sloganeering.

It is quite true that over the years various Labor prime ministers have acted badly towards refugees, and I went to some pains to point that out. If Henderson did not recognise the references as critical, all I can say is that he is even more uptight than I suspected. But no other leader from either side of politics, at least in Henderson's and my lifetimes, has run an election based so heavily on xenophobia, or been so contemptuous of international criticism. Nor would any of those Henderson mentions have dreamt of doing so. This is the charge against Howard. Henderson is normally a zealous opponent of what he calls "moral equivalence". In his attempt to excuse Howard's calculated exploitation of bigotry and prejudice as being on the same level as a few lines of rhetoric from Chifley, Hawke and Whitlam, Henderson is guilty of a particularly nasty example of it himself.

Recent events have shown, yet again, just how dehumanising the government's treatment of asylum seekers has become. Yet comparisons with other international abuses of human rights are dismissed by Howard with lines like "Well, they didn't have to come here," and by Henderson with his all-purpose, favourite sneer: hyperbole.

Which leads to the ritual final insult: if the word "hyperbole" ever disappears from the language, the faceless men of The Sydney Institute will have to buy their mouthpiece a new set of alphabet blocks.

John Hirst essentially accepts the Howard line that the issue is essentially one of border protection, of control of the immigration program. But if this is so, why does the control need to be so draconian? Other countries do not lock up asylum seekers in privatised prison camps behind several barriers of razor wire; they do not say that the only hope for children who have been traumatised by their experiences is to separate them from their parents. And other governments do not tell their citizens that those seeking refuge are dangerous criminals, potential terrorists, fanatics capable of mutilating and even killing their own children. The point is that these are indeed the same sort of people we accept as immigrants; Howard and Ruddock want us to believe that they are another race, another species.

Hirst says that most Australians still favour immigration; attitudes do not change overnight. I am not so sure. The attitude that tolerated, indeed welcomed boat people in the '80s and early '90s seems to me to have changed radically in the last ten years and I suspect there is a hardening view against immigration as a possibly unintended consequence. Certainly the electorate responded to Iron John's assertion of control: "We will decide who comes into this country and the circumstances in which they come." But to see this simply as a statement of sovereignty is to ignore the lengthy campaign of demonisation that led up to it. Howard had identified the enemy; now he was effectively declaring war. And I fear that if he had also declared that he was planning to suspend the immigration program altogether for the duration he would have been greeted with the same enthusiasm. If Hirst missed the mood of xenophobia that underlay the whole campaign, he was one of the few who did so.

Angela Shanahan's contribution bears out the widely held belief that those toughest on new arrivals are themselves part of an earlier wave of immigrants. Shanahan describes her attitude as "cynicism", but surely she is selling herself short; her approach reeks of downright hostility.

Chinese students fearful of going home in the wake of the Tiananmen massacre are dismissed as "the sons and daughters of apparatchiks", and we are told that the Indochinese were accepted only because they (well, at least some of them) were our allies during the American adventure in Vietnam; the implication is that otherwise they would have been unceremoniously rejected, and quite right too.

Angela* believes that xenophobia has always been with us, and rather approves of the idea. Apart from the blemish of Lambing Flat it only went over the top, she claims, not in the current treatment of asylum seekers (whom she insists, wrongly, are "illegals") but in the internment of what were described as "enemy aliens" in World War II, among them her grandfather. I certainly agree that this was a shameful overreaction, albeit one practised equally by England, the United States and Canada. But surely the idea that an immigrant's loyalty to his homeland might make him a potential fifth columnist is no more offensive or fanciful than the present government's insistence that boatloads of those fleeing terrorist

*Normally I find the use of first names in this kind of debate both presumptuous and patronising, but since Mrs Shanahan apparently feels such intimacy appropriate with one she has never met, I feel bound to reciprocate. At least it helps to distinguish her from her husband Dennis who also works for the *Australian*, thus confirming Rupert Murdoch's commitment to the family.

regimes might themselves include terrorists – and this libel, like many others, seems to be unique to Australia.

Angela was understandably distressed at being called a wog at school and hints at other harassment, but states triumphantly: "But so what? We got over it." Well, good for her. But we are not talking about name-calling in a playground; we are talking about razor wire, water cannon, guards with truncheons, madness and attempted suicides. I'm sure Shayan Badraie's playmates in Woomera would be ecstatic at the prospect of an environment in which the worst that happened was that they were teased and bullied by other children. Shayan himself, of course, was eventually liberated as a result of pressure from doctors, psychiatrists and the media; I suppose that makes him a symbol, although I still see him as a little boy who was literally scared to the point of death. It was Philip Ruddock, not the left, who referred to the child as "it".

Angela suspects that her former neighbours in Arncliffe are, like herself, "not too sympathetic" to the Woomera detainees. She is probably right; after all, Howard and his colleagues have spent the last four years telling them how terrible, threatening, evil and above all different the asylum seekers are. It is this, not some mythical cross-cultural charisma, which is the basis for dislike of John Howard; the fact that he is prepared to exploit fear, hate and division simply to keep himself in power. And as Angela shows, it works; she and her friends are quite happy to ignore injustice and suffering as long as they can improve their own material position. This, she crows, makes me and those who hold similar views redundant. A less self-centred conclusion might be that it makes us all the more necessary.

Robyn Spencer is at least straightforward about her bigotry: "Of course early Anglo-European immigration was acceptable because these people immigrated under a policy of assimilation and most importantly were from the same Western Christian civilisation as our own." Those who diverge from this somewhat limited ideal are the enemies of the people: at various points in her diatribe big business, humanitarians, ethnic community leaders, multinationals, bleeding hearts, internationalists, globalisation, governments, the pinko left socialists, the New World Order and, of course, those who favour immigration and multiculturalism. It is indeed an impressive line-up, and one Robyn (who is even chummier than Angela – what have I done to deserve this?) believes is supported by nearly every journalist and media presenter in the land. She has obviously been brought up in a household in which there were no tabloid newspapers, commercial radio or television.

But then, Robyn has led a pretty sheltered life all around; she assures us that the only threat to John Howard at the last election came from her own One

Nation. It is not really possible to debate such assertions; all I can say is that she is entitled to her point of view, even if it is (in Gerard Henderson's felicitous phrase) that of the lunar right.

A final, belated, response came from Immigration Minister Philip Ruddock, or at least from his office. A detailed reply had been promised earlier; when it eventually arrived it proved to be little more than a general media hand-out on government policy without any direct reference to my essay. After repeated requests for something more specific we received the same thing again, but with five paragraphs affixed to the top. They read like a last-minute lawyer's reply, so perhaps Ruddock himself was responsible for at least this bit.

With amazing perspicacity, Ruddock notes that I did not write about displaced person (of course we mustn't call them refugee) camps in Africa, the Middle East or West Asia. This is not true; nor did I write about the American space shuttle, the Greenhouse Effect or prospects for the FIFA World Cup. As the title of my essay suggests, I wrote about Australia, the Refugees and the Politics of Fear. This does not mean I am unaware of everything else in the world, and Ruddock will be pleased to know that I contribute regularly to a number of overseas aid programs including his very own favourite, Amnesty International. But on this basis Ruddock accuses me of naivety and distortion, adding hastily that he does not intend to go to specific instances of either.

He then proceeds to verbal me in a manner which would not be permitted in the courts where he made his name. I have never held up the boat people as "heroes"; I did describe them as desperate, which is not quite the same thing. I have never suggested that "every asylum seeker is a refugee" – although I am surprised to see that Ruddock also insists that it is equally wrong to claim that "every boat arrival is an asylum seeker." If we are talking about "unlawful arrivals" – a term I have never disputed; it is the use of "illegals" to which I object – then just which boat people are not asylum seekers? Perhaps the ones Ruddock's departmental officers dismiss because they cannot find the correct form of words the moment that they land.

This is a piece of sophistry on the same level as Ruddock's assertion that the majority of asylum seekers are not detained but are free in the community. Those accepted as refugees have indeed been released, albeit under temporary protection visas – hardly what ordinary Australians would accept as freedom. As far as I know all those still being processed – all those seeking asylum – are still behind the razor wire. The ones who arrived on the *Tampa* certainly are.

And of course our official immigration policy is not racist. This has not been an argument since at least 1973. But the suspicion is that the present approach to asylum seekers is racist, and that the government has exploited it as such. Ruddock once again ducks the question: if the *Tampa* had been full of white Christian Zimbabwean farmers, would it have been refused permission to land, would the boat have been seized by the SAS, would its passengers have been isolated in hastily prepared camps in other countries? The answer is all too obvious.

The rest of his response is the general statement of policy mentioned above. In it, Ruddock insists that the policy is firm but fair; as a sort of modern-day sea green incorruptible, he must stick to the absolute letter of the law, unmoved by pity or compassion. Thus it is utterly wrong to give preference to those who arrive uninvited, no matter how tragic their plight, because there are always others waiting in the camps who may be in even more desperate circumstances. Treating the asylum seekers in such a manner as to discourage other boat people is simple justice; if it appears cruel, well, there's no real alternative. This reasoning is both heartless and specious; it is the sort of logic that says if you see someone bleeding in the gutter, do nothing about it because there may be someone more gravely in need of the inadequate number of hospital beds available.

As a practising Christian Ruddock will be familiar with the parable of the Good Samaritan: the Samaritan understood that common decency demands that you do what you can when you can, rather than seek refuge in lofty rationalisations. Ruddock and his colleagues in the Howard government, like those other authority figures the priest and the Levite, prefer to pass by on the other side and let the victims suffer as a terrible example to others.

Mungo MacCallum

Alison Broinowski is Visiting Fellow at the Faculty of Asian Studies, Australian National University and the author of *Yellow Lady: Australian Impressions of Asia*.

John Button was Senate Leader of the Hawke and Keating Labor governments from 1983 until his retirement from politics in 1993. Over the same period he was Minister for Industry, Technology and Commerce. He is the author of *Flying the Kite*, *On the Loose* and *As It Happened*.

Gerard Henderson is Executive Director of the Sydney Institute.

John Hirst is Reader in History at La Trobe University and the author of *The Sentimental Nation*.

Mungo MacCallum's collections of political journalism include *Mungo's Canberra* and *Mungo on the Zoo Plane*. His memoir, *Mungo: The Man Who Laughs*, was published in 2001.

Philip Ruddock is the Minister for Immigration and Multicultural and Indigenous Affairs.

Angela Shanahan is a freelance journalist with a regular column in the *Australian*. Her writing has appeared in the *Sydney Telegraph*, the *Sydney Morning Herald*, the *Adelaide Review* and *Quadrant*.

Robyn Spencer is the Immigration, Multicultural and Population Policy Spokesperson for the One Nation Party.

QUARTERLY ESSAY

SUBSCRIPTIONS Receive a discount and never miss an issue. Mailed direct to your door. 1 year subscription (4 issues): $46.95 a year within Australia incl. GST (Institutional subs. $52.95). Outside Australia $74.95. All prices include postage and handling.

BACK ISSUES Please add $2.50 postage and handling to your order (or $8.00 for overseas orders).

- ☐ **Issue 1** ($9.95) Robert Manne's *In Denial: The Stolen Generations and the Right*
- ☐ **Issue 2** ($9.95) John Birmingham's *Appeasing Jakarta: Australia's Complicity in the East Timor Tragedy*
- ☐ **Issue 3** ($9.95) Guy Rundle's *The Opportunist: John Howard and the Triumph of Reaction*
- ☐ **Issue 4** ($9.95) Don Watson's *Rabbit Syndrome: Australia and America*
- ☐ **Issue 5** ($11.95) Mungo MacCallum's *Girt by Sea: Australia, the Refugees and the Politics of Fear*

PAYMENT DETAILS I enclose a cheque/money order made out to Schwartz Publishing Pty Ltd. Please debit my credit card (Mastercard, Visa Card or Bankcard accepted).

Card No. ☐☐☐☐☐☐☐☐☐☐☐☐☐☐☐☐

Expiry date / Amount $

Cardholder's name

Signature

Name

Address

Email

POST OR FAX TO:
Black Inc.
Level 5, 289 Flinders Lane, Melbourne,
Victoria 3000 Australia
Telephone: 61 3 9654 2000
Facsimile: 61 3 9654 2290
Email: quarterlyessay@blackincbooks.com

Black Inc.

Subscribe online at www.blackincbooks.com